Edward Augustus Freeman

A short history of the Norman conquest of England

Second Edition

Edward Augustus Freeman

A short history of the Norman conquest of England
Second Edition

ISBN/EAN: 9783337203269

Printed in Europe, USA, Canada, Australia, Japan

Cover: Foto ©ninafisch / pixelio.de

More available books at **www.hansebooks.com**

THE NORMAN CONQUEST

E. A. FREEMAN

London

HENRY FROWDE

OXFORD UNIVERSITY PRESS WAREHOUSE

7 PATERNOSTER ROW

𝔆𝔩𝔞𝔯𝔢𝔫𝔡𝔬𝔫 𝔓𝔯𝔢𝔰𝔰 𝔖𝔢𝔯𝔦𝔢𝔰

A SHORT HISTORY

OF THE

NORMAN CONQUEST

OF

ENGLAND

BY

EDWARD A. FREEMAN, D.C.L., LL.D.

Honorary Fellow of Trinity College, Oxford
Corresponding Member of the Imperial Academy of Sciences
of Saint Petersburg

Second Edition

𝔒𝔵𝔣𝔬𝔯𝔡

AT THE CLARENDON PRESS

M DCCC LXXX

CONTENTS.

CHAP.		PAGE
I.	INTRODUCTION	1
II.	THE ENGLISH AND THE NORMANS	6
III.	THE EARLY DEALINGS BETWEEN ENGLISH AND NORMANS	16
IV.	THE YOUTH OF DUKE WILLIAM	30
V.	HAROLD EARL AND KING	39
VI.	THE TWO HAROLDS	55
VII.	THE COMING OF DUKE WILLIAM	64
VIII.	THE GREAT BATTLE	76
IX.	HOW DUKE WILLIAM BECAME KING	86
X.	HOW KING WILLIAM WON THE WHOLE KINGDOM	93
XI.	KING WILLIAM'S LATER WARS	108
XII.	HOW KING WILLIAM RULED THE LAND	118
XII.	THE TWO WILLIAMS	128
XIV.	THE RESULTS OF THE NORMAN CONQUEST	134
XV.	THE LATER HISTORY	148

INTRODUCTION.

I have here told, in the shape of a primer, the same tale which I have already told in five large volumes. I have only to say that, though the tale told is the same, yet the little book is not an abridgement of the large one, but strictly the same tale told afresh. I should be well pleased if I am able some day to tell the same tale on a third and intermediate scale.

SOMERLEAZE, WELLS,
June 5, 1880.

THE NORMAN CONQUEST OF ENGLAND.

CHAPTER I.

INTRODUCTION.

1. Meaning of the Norman Conquest.—By the Norman Conquest of England we understand that series of events during the latter part of the eleventh century by which a Norman Duke was set on the throne of England, and was enabled to hand down the crown of England to his descendants. The Norman Conquest of England does in truth mean a great deal more than the mere transfer of the crown from one prince or one family to another, or even than the transfer of the crown from a prince born in the land to a prince who came from beyond sea. It means a great number of changes of all kinds which have made the history and state of our land ever since to be very different from what they would have been if the Norman Conquest had never happened. For the Norman Duke could not be set on the throne of England without making many changes of all kinds in the state of England. But the fact that a Norman Duke was set on the throne of England is the central point of the whole story of the Norman Conquest of England. That story must tell how William Duke of the Normans became William King of the English. It must also tell how it came about that the Norman Duke could be made King of the English; that is, it must tell something of the causes which led to the Norman Conquest. It must also tell of the changes which came through the way in which the Norman Duke was made King of the English. That is, it must tell something of the effects which followed on the Norman Conquest. And, in order to make the causes of the Conquest rightly understood, it must tell something of the state of things among both the Normans and the English before the Norman Conquest of England happened. And, in order to make the effects of the Conquest rightly understood, it must go on to tell something of the times for some while after the Conquest itself, that we may see the way in which the changes which followed on the Conquest were wrought, and how they have had an effect on English history ever since.

2. **Meaning of the word Conquest.**—We may now ask a little further what is the meaning of the word *conquest*, whether there can be more kinds of conquest than one, and whether the Norman Conquest of England has anything about it which is either like or unlike any other conquest. Now the word *conquest* strictly means the winning or getting of anything, whether rightly or not, or whether by force or not. It might mean, for instance, the winning of land, whether a kingdom or anything smaller, by strength of war, or it might mean winning it by sentence of law. And this first meaning of the word has something specially to do with the Norman Conquest of England. For when King William was called the *Conqueror*, it did not at first mean that he had won the crown of England by force; for he claimed it as his own by law. But as, though he claimed it as his own by law, he had in fact to win it by force, we can also rightly speak of the *Conquest* and the *Conqueror* in the sense which those words now commonly bear, that of winning a land and the rule over it by strength of war. For, though Duke William claimed the crown as

his own by law, he could get it only by coming into our land with an army and overthrowing and killing our king in fight, and when he had got the crown and was called King, he had still to win the land bit by bit, often by hard fighting, before he had really got the whole kingdom into his hands. The Norman Conquest of England was therefore a conquest in the best known meaning of the word; it was the winning of the land by strength of war.

3. **Different kinds of Conquests.**—Now this fact that Duke William claimed the English crown as his own by law, and yet had to win it in battle at the head of a foreign army, had a great deal to do with the special character of the Norman Conquest of England, and with the effect which that Conquest has had on the history of England ever since. There have been at different times conquests of very different kinds. Sometimes a whole people has gone from one land to another; they have settled by force in a land where other men were dwelling, and have killed or driven out the men whom they found in the land, or have let them live on as bondmen in their own land. Here is mere force without any pretence of right, and a conquest like this can happen only among people who are quite uncivilized, as we English were when we first came to the island of Britain. The Norman Conquest was nothing at all like this; the English were neither killed nor driven out nor made slaves, but went on living in their own land as before. The Norman Conquest was, so to speak, less of a conquest than conquests of this kind. But it was much more of a conquest than some other conquests of another kind have been. In some conquests of later times all that has happened has been something of this kind. A king has won a kingdom by force, or he has added some new lands to the kingdom which he had

before. The changes made by such a conquest may be only what we may call political changes, changes in the government and most likely to some extent in the law. Such a conquest may be made with very little change which directly touches private men; it may be made without turning anybody out of his house or land. Indeed many men may even keep on the public offices which they held before. Now the Norman Conquest of England, though not so much as the other kind of conquest, was much more than this. For though the English nation was not killed or driven out, yet very many Englishmen had their lands, houses, and offices taken from them and given to strangers. And this happened specially with the greatest estates and the highest offices. These passed almost wholly to strangers. It was not merely that a foreign king won the English crown, but that his foreign followers displaced Englishmen in nearly all the highest places in the English kingdom.

4. **Nature of the Norman Conquest.**—Now this special character of the Norman Conquest of England, as being more than one kind of conquest and less than another, came chiefly of the fact that a prince who claimed the English crown by law did in truth win it by force of arms. No one in England supported his claim; he had to make it good at the head of a foreign army. And when he had thus won the crown, he had at once to make himself safe in the strange land which he had conquered, and to reward those who had helped him to conquer it. He therefore very largely took away the lands and offices of the English who had fought against him, and gave them to the Normans and other strangers who had fought for him. But, as he claimed to be king reigning according to law, he gave them those lands and offices to be held of the English crown, according to English law. From this, and from many

other causes, it came about that the descendants of the Normans who settled in England step by step become, as we may say, Englishmen, if not by blood yet by adoption. For several generations after the Conquest the high places of the land, the great estates and chief offices, were almost always held by men of Norman or other foreign blood. But in a very few generations these men learned to speak English and to have the feelings of Englishmen. The effect of the Norman Conquest of England was neither to make England subject to Normandy nor to make it a Norman land. It gave to England a much higher place in the world in general than it had held before. At home, Englishmen were neither driven out nor turned into Normans, but the Normans in England were turned into Englishmen. But in this work of turning themselves into Englishmen, they made, bit by bit, many changes in the laws of England, and in the language, manners, and thoughts of Englishmen.

5. **Causes of the Norman Conquest.**—We have thus seen what kind of a work the Norman Conquest of England was, as compared with other conquests of our own and of other lands. It is well thoroughly to understand this in a general way before we begin to tell our tale at all at length. And before we come to tell the tale of the Conquest itself, we must try clearly to understand what kind of people both Englishmen and Normans were at the time when the Normans crossed the sea to conquer England. We must see what were the real causes, and what were the immediate occasions, which led to an event which seems so strange as that a Norman Duke should give out that he had a right to the English crown, and that he should actually be able to win it by war. And to do this, we must run lightly over the history both of the English and of the Normans down to the time when they first began to have any dealings with one another.

CHAPTER II.

The English and the Normans.

1. The English and Norman Settlements.—When the Normans crossed the sea to conquer England, the English had been much longer settled in the land which from them was called England than the Normans had been in the land which from them was called Normandy. It was in the fifth century that the English began to settle in those parts of the isle of Britain which from them took the name of England. But it was not till the beginning of the tenth century that the Normans settled in that part of the mainland of Gaul which from them took the name of Normandy. The English had thus been living for six hundred years in their land, when the Normans had been living only about a hundred and fifty years in theirs. The English therefore in the eleventh century were more thoroughly at home in England than the Normans were in Normandy. The adventurous spirit of new settlers had spent itself among the English in the long wars with the Welsh which established the English dominion in Britain. But in the Normans that spirit was still quite fresh. Their conquest of England was only one, though it was the greatest, of several conquests in foreign lands made by the Normans about this time. Both were brave; but the courage of the English was of the passive kind with which men defend their old homes; the courage of the Normans was of the restless, ambitious, kind with which men go forth to seek for themselves new homes.

2. The English in Britain.—The first time when the affairs of Normandy and of England came to have anything to do with one another was about eighty years before the Norman Conquest of England. At that time all England was united into one kingdom under the kings of the house of the West-Saxons. In the course of about a hundred years after their first landing, the English had founded seven or eight chief kingdoms, besides smaller states, at the expense of the Welsh, occupying all the eastern and central parts of Britain. Among these states four stand out as of special importance, as having at different times seemed likely to win the chief power over all their neighbours. These were Kent, Wessex, Mercia, and Northumberland. The power of Kent came early to an end, but for a long time it seemed very doubtful to which of the other three the chief power would come. Sometimes one had the upper hand, and sometimes another. But at last, in the early years of the ninth century, the West-Saxon king Ecgberht won the chief power over all the English kingdoms and over all the Welsh in the southern part of the island. The northern parts of the island, inhabited by the Picts, the Scots, and the northern Welsh, remained quite independent. And in the English and southern Welsh kingdoms kings went on reigning, though the West-Saxon king was their *lord* and they were his *men*. That is, though he had nothing to do with the internal affairs of their kingdoms, they were to follow him in matters of peace and war, and at all events never to fight against him. Long before the chief lordship thus came into the hands of the West-Saxon kings, all the English kingdoms had embraced Christianity. Kent was the first to do so; its conversion began at the end of the sixth century (597), and all England had become Christian before the end of the seventh.

3. **The Danes in England.**—Not long after the West-Saxon kings had won the chief power over the other English kingdoms, a series of events began which made a great change in England, and which was of a truth the beginning of the Normans as a people. The people of Scandinavia, the Danes and the Northmen or Norwegians, began about this time, first to plunder and then to settle both in England and in Gaul. They were still heathens, just as the English had been when they first landed in Britain. Their invasions were therefore the more frightful, and they took special delight in destroying the churches and monasteries. In England all the latter part of the ninth century is taken up with the story of their ravaging and settlements. They settled in eastern and northern England; they overran Wessex for a moment, but there they were defeated and driven out by the famous King Alfred. They had upset the other English kingdoms, so that Wessex was now the only independent English and Christian kingdom. Alfred could therefore treat with them as the one English king. The Danish king Guthrum was baptized, and a line was drawn between his dominions and those of Alfred, leaving to Alfred all Wessex and the other lands south of the Thames and all south-western Mercia. Thus Alfred lost as an over-lord; but his own kingdom was enlarged; and the coming of the Danes, by uprooting the other English kingdoms, opened the way for the West-Saxon Kings to win the whole of England. This was done under Alfred's successors, Edward, Æthelstan, Edmund, and Eadred, in the first half of the tenth century. After long fighting, all the English kingdoms were won from the Danes and were united to the kingdom of the West-Saxons. And

the Kings of the English, as they were now called, held the lordship over the other kingdoms of Britain, Scottish and Welsh.

4. **The Northmen in Gaul.**—While this was going on in Britain, something of much the same kind was going on in Gaul. Throughout the ninth century the Northmen were plundering in Gaul, sailing up the rivers, burning towns and monasteries, and sometimes making small settlements here and there. But in the beginning of the tenth century they made a much greater and more lasting settlement. A colony of Northmen settled in that part of Gaul which from them took the name of Normandy, and there founded a new European state. This was in the year 912. The great dominion of the Franks under Charles the Great was now quite broken up into four kingdoms. That of the West-Franks, called *Karolingia*, because several of its kings bore the name of Charles, took in the greater part of Gaul. The crown was more than once disputed between the kings of the house of Charles the Great, who reigned at Laon, and the Dukes of the French, whose capital was Paris, and whose duchy of *France* was the greatest state of Gaul north of the Loire. Some of these dukes themselves wore the crown, and, when they did not, they were much more powerful than the kings at Laon. But whether the king reigned at Paris or Laon, the princes south of the Loire, though they called themselves his men, took very little heed to him. Now when the kingdom was at Laon, the king was pretty well out of the way of invaders who came by sea; but no part of Gaul was more exposed than the duchy of France, with its long seaboard on the Channel, and with the mouth of the river Seine making a highway for the Northmen up to Rouen and Paris. Paris was several times besieged in the ninth century; and now at the beginning of the tenth, the coasts

of Gaul, especially the northern coast, were ravaged by a great pirate-leader named Rolf—called in Latin *Rollo* and in French *Rou*—who had got possession of Rouen and seemed disposed to settle in the land.

5. Settlement of Rolf.—At this time the kingdom of the West-Franks was held by Charles, called the Simple, who reigned at Laon. Robert, Duke of the French, was his man, but a man much more powerful than his lord. But no prince in Gaul had suffered so much from Rolf's ravages. So King Charles and Duke Robert agreed that the best thing to be done was very much what Alfred had done with Guthrum, to grant to Rolf part of the land as his own, if he would be baptized and hold it as the man of the king. So Rolf was baptized with Duke Robert to his godfather, and he took his name in baptism, though he was still commonly spoken of as Rolf. And he received the city of Rouen and the land from the Epte to the Dive, as a fief from King Charles, and became his man. So Rolf and his followers settled down in the land which from them was called the *Land of the Northmen* and afterwards the Duchy of Normandy. It was enlarged in Rolf's own time by the addition of the city of Bayeux and its territory, and in the time of his son William Longsword, by the addition of the peninsular land of Coutances, called the *Côtentin*, and the land of Avranches to the south of it. The Norman dukes claimed also to be lords over the counties of Britanny and Maine; but they could never really make good their power there. But the whole north coast of the duchy of France now became the duchy of Normandy. Paris and its prince, sometimes king, sometimes only duke, were quite cut off from the sea by the land of the Norman dukes at Rouen.

6. The Early Norman Dukes.—In this lay the beginning of the strife between Normandy and France, which, when the same princes came to rule over England and Normandy, grew into the long wars between France and England. The princes and people of France never forgot that they had lost the great city of Rouen and all the fair land of Normandy. But King Charles at Laon gained by the duchy of France being in this way weakened and cut in two. He gained too because, when Rolf swore to be his man and be faithful to him, he really kept his oath. For when first Duke Robert of France (922), and then Duke Rudolf of Burgundy (923), rose up against King Charles and were made kings in his stead, both Rolf and his son William after him clave to the lord to whom Rolf had first sworn. Rolf too ruled his land well, and put down thieves and murderers, so that the story ran that he hung up a jewel in a tree, and no man dared to take it. Under him and his son William Longsword (927–943) most of the Normans gradually became Christians, and left off their Scandinavian tongue and learned to speak French. By the end of William's reign nothing but French was spoken at Rouen; but in the lands to the west, which had been won more lately, men still spoke Danish, and many still clave to the gods of the North. This heathen and Danish party more than once revolted, and, after the death of Duke William, they even for a while got hold of the young Duke Richard and made him join in their heathen worship. About the same time new settlements from the North were made in the Côtentin. But Duke Richard presently commended himself to Hugh the Great, Duke of the French; that is, he became his man instead of the King's man. During the rest of his reign the duchies of France and Normandy were in close alliance, and Richard had a chief hand in giving the kingdom to Hugh Capet, the son of Hugh the Great.

7. **Manners of the Normans.**—During Richard's reign then the Normans were getting more and more French in

their language and manners. And more than this, it was their help which took the crown of Karolingia from the German kings at Laon, and gave it to the French kings at Paris. Thus the Dukes of the French became Kings of the French, and, as they extended their power, the name of their duchy of *France* was gradually spread over nearly all Karolingia, and over the greater part of the rest of Gaul. In the time of the next Duke, Richard the Good (996–1026), there was a great revolt of the peasants in Normandy. These were most likely largely of Celtic descent, while all the great landowners were Normans. And it is also noticed of this duke that he began to draw new distinctions among his subjects, and would have none but *gentlemen* about him. This is almost the first time that we hear that word. The peasants were put down, and the gentlemen had the upper hand. The Normans had now quite changed from the ways of their Northern forefathers. From seafaring men they had turned into the best horsemen in the world. The Norman gentleman, mounted on his horse, with his shield like a kite, his long lance, and sometimes his sword or mace-at-arms, became the best of all fighting-men of his own kind. And, now that they were fully settled in their own land, the Normans began, quite in the spirit of their forefathers, though in another garb, to go all over the world to seek for fighting wherever fighting was to be had. Often religious zeal was mingled with love of fighting. Some went to help the Christians of Spain against the Saracens, and others, later in the century, went to help the Eastern Emperors against the Turks. But their greatest exploits of all were done in the two greatest of European islands, one the greatest in the Mediterranean, the other the greatest in the Ocean, Sicily and Britain.

8. **The Normans in Italy and Sicily.**—We shall

come presently to their doings in our own island. But it is well to remark that the Norman Conquest of England was no doubt largely suggested by the Norman exploits in southern Italy and Sicily. These went on during nearly the whole of the eleventh century; but they began under Richard the Good. They were not enterprises of the Norman dukes, or of the Norman state in any way, but of private Norman gentlemen who went out to seek their fortunes. They founded more than one principality in southern Italy, but the most famous settlement was that made by the sons of a simple Norman gentleman called Tancred of Hauteville. They conquered all southern Italy, putting an end to the dominion of the Eastern Emperors, and they got the Pope to invest them with what they conquered. Then Robert Wiscard son of Tancred became Duke of Apulia. He then went on to attack the Eastern Emperor beyond the Hadriatic, and actually held Durazzo and other possessions there for some while. Thence he came back to help the Pope against the Western Emperor Henry the Fourth, so that he defeated both Emperors in one year. His brother Roger, partly with his help, conquered all Sicily from the Mahometans. He was only called Great Count; but his son, another Roger, became the first King of Sicily. All this began before the Norman Conquest of England, and was going on at the same time. We speak of it here to show what manner of men the Normans of the eleventh century were. When private men could found duchies and kingdoms and put Emperors to flight, we might indeed look for great things whenever a Duke of the Normans at the head of his whole people should put forth his full strength.

9. **The Danish Conquest of England.**—Meanwhile the Danish invasions of England, which had been put an end to by the great kings who followed Alfred, began

again in the last twenty years of the tenth century, and went on for thirty-six years (980–1016) till England was altogether conquered. But these were invasions of another kind from the earlier Danish invasions. In the ninth century both England and Denmark were still made up of various settlements, more or less distinct, and this or 'that party of Danish adventurers came to settle in this or that part of England. But in the course of the tenth century Denmark, like England, had been joined together into one kingdom; and the invasions now took the form of an enterprise of a king of all Denmark trying to win the crown of all England. But, though England was now joined under one king, its different parts were not yet thoroughly worked together, and it needed a great king to make the whole force of the kingdom act together. In the former part of the tenth century England had had such great kings; but when the Danish invasions began again, she had a king, Æthelred, of quite another kind. His name means *noble rede* or counsel, but men called him the *Unready* or man without *rede*. For, though he sometimes had what we may call fits of energy, they were commonly in the wrong place; and during his long reign it was only once towards the very end that he showed himself as at all a national leader against the enemy. Generally the Danes landed at this or that point; then, if the men of that shire had a brave leader, a good fight was made against them; but there was no general resistance. The king thought more of giving the Danes money to go away than of fighting them. And of course this only led them to come again for more money. In this way one shire after another was harried; the land was weakened bit by bit, till the Danes could march where they pleased, even in the inland parts. At last, in 1013, the Danish king Swen or Swegen was able to subdue all England, and to make the English acknowledge him as king. King Æthelred had to flee from the land and to take shelter beyond the sea. And his wife and her children had to seek for shelter beyond the sea along with him. By this time the story of Normandy and the story of England are beginning to be joined into one. For Æthelred's wife was a Norman woman, and the land in which he and she sought shelter was her own land of Normandy. We must now therefore go back a little way in our story, and see how the Normans and the English had already come to have dealings with one another, in war and in peace.

CHAPTER III.

THE EARLY DEALINGS BETWEEN ENGLISH AND NORMANS.

1. **Early Dealings between England and Gaul.**—Up to the tenth century the English had very little to do with their neighbours in Gaul. The English kings commonly married the daughters of other English kings, or, after there was only one kingdom, the daughters of their own great men. It was somewhat more common for English kings to give their daughters to foreign kings; but even this did not happen very often. But in the days of Edward the Elder and his son Æthelstan several of Edward's daughters were married to the chief princes of Western Europe. Among them one married King Charles of Laon and another Duke Hugh of Paris. Thus King Lewis the son of Charles was sister's son to the English kings Æthelstan and Edmund. They played a certain part in the affairs of Gaul on behalf of their nephew, and, as Lewis was an enemy of the Normans, it may be that some ill-feeling between the English and the Normans began thus early. But there was no open quarrel till the last years of the tenth century, when Æthelred was King of the English, and towards the end of the long reign of Richard the Fearless in Normandy.

2. **The first Quarrel between England and Normandy.**—The first time when Englishmen and Normans are distinctly recorded to have met as enemies was in a quarrel

which arose out of the Danish invasions of England. In 991 King Æthelred and Duke Richard had a quarrel, and they were made friends by Pope John the Fifteenth. The ground of quarrel seems to have been that the Danes had been allowed to sell the plunder of England in the Norman havens. About nine years later we hear of another quarrel. The Norman writers say that Æthelred sent a fleet with orders to harry the whole land and to bring Duke Richard before him with his hands tied behind his back. Then they tell us that the English fleet did land in the Côtentin, but that they were driven back by the men of the land, with the women helping them, without any help from Duke Richard. We cannot believe these details, any more than we can believe the details of many other stories of these times; but there must be some ground for the tale. At any rate there is no doubt that Æthelred in 1002 married Emma, the daughter of Duke Richard. This was most likely when peace was made, and some say that Æthelred went over to Normandy himself to bring home his bride.

3. **The Marriage of Æthelred and Emma.**—This marriage marks one of the main stages in the events which led to the Norman Conquest. First of all, it was, as we have seen, an unusual thing for an English king to marry a foreign wife. In all the time that the English had been in Britain it had, as far as we know, happened only twice before. This is one of many things which show that England was now getting to have more to do with foreign lands than before. Secondly, by reason of this marriage Normans and other French-speaking people now began for the first time to settle in England and to hold English offices. Emma now became Lady of the English, for by the custom of the West-Saxons the King's wife was called not *Queen* but *Lady*, and she changed her name from the foreign Emma to

the English Ælfgifu. As the King's wife she received a gift from her husband. This gift consisted of lands and towns, and among them the city of Exeter. Here the Lady set one Hugh, whom the English call the French churl, as her reeve. When the Danes attacked Exeter in 1003, Hugh, if he did not actually betray the city, at least made no good defence, and the city was taken. Such was the beginning of Norman command in England. Thirdly, for the first time in the West-Saxon house, the children of a king were half-strangers by birth, and what followed made them strangers yet more thoroughly. And fourthly, the reigning houses of England and Normandy now became of kin to one another, and it was this which first put it into the head of Duke William that he might perhaps succeed to the throne of his English kinsfolk.

4. **The Marriage of Cnut and Emma.**—Emma, the Norman Lady, now becomes a very important person in English history. She was the wife of two kings and the mother of two kings. Her first husband Æthelred had not to stay very long in his banishment in Normandy. For the next year Swegen the Danish king died. Then the Danes chose his younger son Cnut or Canute to be king in England, while his elder son Harold reigned in Denmark. War followed between Cnut and Æthelred, in which at last Æthelred showed some little spirit, but in which the great leader on the English side was his son Edmund, called Ironside. He was not the son of Emma, whose children, Alfred, Edward, and Godgifu, were still quite young, but of an earlier wife of Æthelred. Then in the beginning of 1016 Æthelred died. Many of the English now thought that it was best to accept Cnut as king; so he was chosen at a meeting at Southampton, while Edmund was chosen in another meeting in London. The English gradually joined

Edmund; he was a strong and brave captain, very unlike his father; six battles were fought in the year; London was three times besieged by Cnut; but in the last battle, at Assandún in Essex, Edmund was defeated by the treason of his brother-in-law Eadric. Still he was so powerful that it was agreed to divide the kingdom, Cnut reigning in the North and Edmund in the South. But before the year was out, Edmund died, and many thought that Eadric, some that Cnut, had brought about his death. Then at the Christmas of 1016-1017 Cnut was a third time chosen king over all England, and one of the first things that he did was to send to Normandy for the widowed Lady Emma, though she was many years older than he was. She came over; she married the new king, and was again Lady of the English. She bore Cnut two children, Harthacnut and Gunhild. Her three children by Æthelred were left in Normandy. She seems not to have cared at all for them or for the memory of Æthelred; her whole love passed to her new husband and her new children. Thus it came about that the children of Æthelred were brought up in Normandy, and had the feelings of Normans rather than of Englishmen, a thing which again greatly helped the Norman Conquest.

5. **The Reign of Cnut.**—Though Cnut came in as a foreign conqueror, yet he reigned as an English king. He was chosen when he was quite young; England was his first kingdom; and, though he soon inherited the kingdom of Denmark and afterwards conquered Norway, yet England was always the land which he loved best. He began harshly, banishing or putting to death every one whom he thought at all dangerous, especially such of the kinsfolk of Æthelred as he could get at. Emma's two boys were safe in Normandy, perhaps safer with their uncle Duke Richard—that is Richard

the Good, son of Richard the Fearless, who reigned from 996 to 1026—than they would have been with their mother in England. But when Cnut was fully established on the throne, he left off this harshness; he ruled the English according to their own laws, and gradually got rid of the Danes who had come with him, and to whom he had given earldoms and other high offices. These places were now again given to Englishmen, and the chief among them was Godwine, Earl of the West-Saxons. Under Cnut England became the centre of a great Northern Empire, such as was not seen before or after. His father Swegen had been baptized in his childhood; but he cast away Christianity and became a heathen again. His son Cnut was therefore brought up as a heathen, but he was baptized while still a young man by the name of Lambert, though he was always called Cnut, just as Rolf was always called Rolf and never Robert. He made the pilgrimage to Rome, and was there received with great worship by the Pope and by the Emperor Conrad, who came to be crowned while he was there. All his wars were in the North, in Scotland, Norway, and Sweden. He was always on good terms with Duke Richard of Normandy; but things changed in this respect before the end of Cnut's reign. When Richard the Good died, he was succeeded by his son Richard the Third, who reigned only two years. Then in 1028 came his other son Robert, who is famous in several ways, but perhaps more than all for being the father of William the Conqueror of England.

6. **Duke Robert and the English Æthelings.**—There seems no doubt that Cnut and Robert had some kind of quarrel, but the story is told in different ways, and it is not easy to make out the exact truth. But it seems that Robert married Cnut's sister Estrith and then put her away. She had, seemingly before this, been married to the Danish

Earl Ulf, who was put to death by Cnut, and she was the mother of Swegen called from her *Estrithson*, who was afterwards King of the Danes, and who plays a great part in English history also. The Northern writers tell some wild stories about Cnut invading Normandy and dying while besieging Rouen; but it is quite certain that he died quietly at Shaftesbury in 1035. But it does seem likely that Robert, though he never actually invaded England, yet made ready to do so. He played a great part in the affairs of the neighbouring states, and he seems to have been specially pleased to restore dispossessed princes to their dominions. Thus he restored Baldwin Count of Flanders and his own lord Henry King of the French. He was therefore very likely, above all if he had any quarrel with Cnut on other grounds, to try to bring home his cousins, the English *Æthelings* or King's sons, Alfred and Edward, and to set one of them on the English throne. It is said that he got together a fleet and set out, but he was hindered by the wind, and driven to the coast of Britanny, where he hardly had a quarrel with the reigning Count Alan. So, instead of conquering the greater Britain, of which England is part, all that he did was to harry the lesser Britain in Gaul. But no doubt this attempt of Duke Robert's would make an invasion of England to be talked of in Normandy as a possible thing, and might specially help to put it into the head of his son William.

7. **The Second attempt of the Æthelings.**—Of the accession and youth of William we shall say more presently. It is enough to say now that Cnut and Robert died nearly at the same time. After Cnut's death the kingdom of England was again divided, as it had been before between Edmund and Cnut. Earl Godwine and the West-Saxons wished to keep the whole kingdom for Emma's son Harthacnut, who was already reigning in Denmark under his

father. But it was decreed that Harthacnut should have Wessex only, and that the rest of England, together, it would seem, with the overlordship of all, should pass to Harold, who was said to be Cnut's son by an Englishwoman named Ælfgifu. But Harthacnut stayed in Denmark, and his English kingdom was ruled by his mother Emma, with Godwine to her minister. Thus we seem to be getting nearer to the Norman Conquest, when the Norman Lady rules in Wessex. And now comes a story which is told in the most opposite ways by the old writers. It is certain that one or both of the English Æthelings, Alfred and Edward, made another attempt to get the kingdom of England, that Alfred fell into the hands of Harold, that his eyes were put out by Harold's orders, and that he soon afterwards died. But as to all the details of the story, there is nothing but contradiction. Some say that Edward invaded England with a Norman fleet, and won a battle near Southampton, but sailed away without doing anything more. Others say nothing about Eadward and only speak of Alfred. And it was believed by many that Earl Godwine betrayed Alfred to Harold, though those who say this seem to have forgotten that Godwine was the minister of Harthacnut. Some say too that Alfred had a large party of Normans with him, and that they were put to death in various cruel ways. The chief thing for our purpose is that it was fully believed in Normandy that either Godwine by himself, or the English people with Godwine at their head, had betrayed and murdered the Ætheling, the kinsman of the Norman Duke. So this was treasured up as a ground for vengeance against the English nation in general and against Godwine above all.

8. **Emma and Edward.**—The next thing that happened in England was not likely to please the Normans much better. For the West-Saxons got tired of waiting for their king Har-

thacnut, who stayed all the time in Denmark; so in 1037 they forsook him and chose Harold to be king over Wessex as well as over the rest of England. The first thing that Harold did was to drive the Lady Emma out of the land. She did not go to Normandy, but to Flanders; because Normandy was just then, as we shall presently see, full of confusion. But in 1040 Harold died, and Harthacnut was chosen king over all England. Thus England had a king who was, on the mother's side, of Norman descent. Emma came back, and Harthacnut sent for his half-brother Edward to come from Normandy and live at his court. And Edward brought with him a French nephew of his and of Harthacnut's. This was Ralph, the son of their sister Godgifu or Goda, daughter of Æthelred and Emma, who was married to a French prince, Drogo Count of Mantes. So the foreign influence, Norman and French, was spreading. Their other sister Gunhild, the daughter of Cnut and Emma, was married to King Henry of Germany, afterwards the great Emperor Henry the Third. Harthacnut, like his brother Harold, reigned only a short time, and died in 1042. Then the English said that they had had enough of strange kings, and that they would have a king of the old stock. There were only two men of that stock now living. Edmund Ironside had left two little twin sons, Edmund and Edward, who were sent away beyond sea in Cnut's time. Of these Edmund was dead, but Edward was living far away in Hungary. By modern law he would have been the right heir, as the son of the elder brother. But in those days it was deemed enough to choose within the kingly house, without thinking of any particular rule of succession. So no one thought of Edward who was away in Hungary, and the Wise Men—the great men of the land in their assembly— chose Edward who was near at hand, the son of Æthelred and Emma. Some were for choosing another Danish king, Swegen, the son of Cnut's sister Estrith. Swegen afterwards reigned very wisely in Denmark, and it might perhaps have really been the best thing to choose him. But the feeling was all in favour of a king of the old English stock; so Edward was chosen.

9. **King Edward.**—With Edward's election the connexion between English and Norman affairs becomes closer still; we might almost say that the Norman Conquest began in his time. Men thought that, by choosing Edward, the English royal house was restored to the crown; but it was in truth very much as if a Norman king had been chosen. Harthacnut had as much Norman blood in him as Edward, but he had not been brought up in Normandy; his feelings and ways were Danish. But Edward's feelings and ways were all Norman. His being the son of a Norman mother had not much to do with it, as there was no great love between mother and son. Emma had quite neglected her children by Æthelred, and she seems even to have opposed Edward's election. He had not been very long king before he took away all her treasures. What really made Edward more of a Norman than an Englishman was that he lived in Normandy from his childhood, and had made many friends there, and chiefly his young cousin Duke William. He liked to speak French and to have French-speaking people about him, specially Norman churchmen, to whom he gave English bishoprics and other high preferments. He also gave estates and offices to Norman and other French-speaking laymen as far as he could; but the King could not give away the great temporal offices so much according to his own pleasure as he could give away the great places of the Church. He could not give away either without the consent of his Wise Men; but the Wise Men were

more ready to allow a foreign bishop than a foreign earl. So, while we find several French-speaking bishops and abbots in Edward's reign, we find only one French-speaking earl. This was the King's nephew Ralph the son of Godgifu. Of smaller men, both clergy and laymen, there were many holding benefices and estates. This was specially so during the former part of Edward's reign, which was chiefly a time of struggle between English and foreign influences in the land.

10. **King Edward and Earl Godwine.**—Edward was a devout and well-disposed man. His love of foreigners he could hardly help; his chief fault was now and then giving way to fits of passion, in which he sometimes gave rash and cruel orders. But in these cases he seems to have been commonly stirred up by his favourites. Otherwise he was remarkably free from cruelty or any other of the common vices of his time. Being thus a really good and pious man, and one whom both Normans and English could agree in reverencing, he was very early looked on as a saint and thought to work miracles. But he was a weak man and quite unfit to govern his kingdom. The first nine years of his reign were one long struggle whether England should be ruled by the King's foreign favourites or by the English Earl Godwine. Godwine, along with his friend Bishop Lyfing, had the chief hand in bringing about Eadward's election, and this claim on the King's gratitude made him yet more the first man in the kingdom than he was before. The King married his daughter Edith, and his sons were gradually raised to earldoms, some of them while they were very young. Godwine was beyond all doubt an Englishman who loved his own land and folk; but he was over-grasping on his own behalf and on that of his children. In marrying his daughter to the King, he no doubt looked forward to a grandson of his own wearing the crown; but Edward had

no children, and, at least in the early part of his reign, he seems to have had little love for his wife. And the gathering together of many earldoms in the one house of the Earl of the West-Saxons gave offence, not only to the Normans, but seemingly to the earls and people of the rest of England. Thus these first years of the reign of Eadward tell us the tale both of the power of Godwine and of his fall.

11. **The Earldoms.**—It will be well here to explain who were the chief men of England at this time, and what were the earldoms which they held. At this time an earldom was not a mere rank or title, but meant the government of one or more shires over which the earl was set by the authority of the King and his Wise Men. There were now four chief earldoms, answering to the four greatest of the ancient kingdoms, those of Wessex, Mercia, Northumberland, and East-Anglia. There were always these four; but there were also others as well, and shires were often taken from one earldom and given to another, as was thought good at the time. The Mercian shires above all, those in the middle of England, were very often handed to and fro between one earl and another. When Edward was elected, Godwine was Earl of the West-Saxons, that is, of all England south of the Thames. Siward, a famous Dane, was Earl of the Northumbrians, that is of all England north of the Humber and the Ribble, and also of Northamptonshire and Huntingdonshire. Leofric was Earl of the Mercians, but he had only the western part of Mercia under his immediate rule. Who was Earl of the East-Angles we do not know. Besides these there were other earls who held one or more shires, seemingly under the great earls; and as these smaller earldoms became vacant, room was found both for the King's friends and for the family of Godwine. Thus the King's nephew Ralph was Earl, first of Worcester and then of Hereford. And Godwine very soon got earldoms for his

elder sons Swegen and Harold, and for his wife's nephew Beorn, the brother of the Danish King Swegen. Swegen had a strangely-shaped government, taking in Somerset, Gloucestershire, Herefordshire, Berkshire, and Oxfordshire. Harold had East-Anglia; Beorn had all eastern Mercia except Northamptonshire and Huntingdonshire. Thus the power of Godwine and his house was very great; but it was perhaps shaken by the crimes of his eldest son Swegen, who killed his cousin Beorn. For this he was banished, but was afterwards restored to his earldom.

12. **Norman influence in England.**—The way in which Godwine had to strive against the King's love of strangers is shown, as we have said, in the appointment of bishoprics and other great offices in the Church. Early in his reign, in 1044, the see of London was given to Robert, Abbot of Jumièges in Normandy, the first time that an English bishopric had ever been held by a French-speaking man. Robert had great power over the King, which he used against the English and especially against Godwine. At last in 1051 Robert himself became Archbishop of Canterbury; other bishoprics were given to Normans, and Norman clerks and knights held benefices and estates in various parts of the kingdom. But the King did not venture to give an earldom to any Norman, or to any foreigner except his own nephew Ralph. One fashion which the Normans brought in with them was that of building castles. The English were used to fortify towns, and their kings and other chief men had lived in *halls*, often on the tops of mounds and fenced in by a palisade. But the Normans now began to build *castles*, that is, either strong square towers, or strong stone walls crowning the mounds. Thence they could oppress the people in many ways, and the writers of the time always speak of the building of the castles with a kind of shudder.

13. The Banishment of Godwine.—The appointment of Robert to the archbishopric marks the time when the Normans had things most thoroughly their own way. About this time the King's brother-in-law, Count Eustace of Boulogne, came to pay him a visit. As he went home, he and his followers rode into the town of Dover, and tried to quarter themselves where they pleased in the houses. So a fight followed, in which several men were killed on both sides. Then the Count rode back and told the King how insolently the men of Dover had dealt by him. Then Edward flew into one of his angry fits, and bade Godwine go and lay waste Dover with fire and sword. But Godwine said that he would do no such thing; he would do nothing to any man in his earldom except according to law; the men of Dover should be lawfully tried before the Wise Men, and, if they were found guilty of any crime, they should be lawfully punished. While these things were doing in Kent, there came also a cry from Herefordshire about the deeds of certain Normans there, Richard and his son Osbern, who had built a castle called *Richard's Castle*, and had greatly oppressed the people. And at the same time the Archbishop and the other Normans were setting the King more against Godwine than ever, and bringing up the old story about his brother Alfred. Godwine and his sons therefore gathered the men of their earldoms, and demanded that the King should give up the foreigners, Count Eustace among them, for lawful trial. Edward got together the forces of the rest of the kingdom under the Earls Siward, Leofric, and Ralph, and made ready for war. The West-Saxons and East-Angles accordingly marched on Gloucester, where the King was; but actual warfare was hindered by Leofric, and it was agreed that all matters should be judged in an assembly in London. The King came there with an army. The assembly met; Swegen's outlawry was renewed; Godwine and Harold were summoned to appear as criminals for trial. As they refused to come without a safe-conduct, they were outlawed. Harold and Leofwine found shelter in Ireland, Godwine and the rest of the family in Flanders. The King's wife, the Lady Edith, stayed in England, but she was shorn of her royal rank, and sent to the monastery of Wherwell. The Normans now had for awhile everything their own way. They thought it a good time for Duke William to come over and pay a visit to his cousin the King. William was now about twenty-three years of age, and he had been called Duke ever since he was a child of seven. We will now go back and see what had been going on in Normandy during these early years of his reign.

CHAPTER IV.

THE YOUTH OF DUKE WILLIAM.

1. The Birth and Accession of Duke William.— WE have already spoken of Duke Robert, and how he tried to bring back his cousins the Æthelings to England. Towards the end of his reign Duke Robert determined to go on a pilgrimage to Jerusalem, to pray at the tomb of Christ and win the forgiveness of his sins. Before he went, he wished to settle the succession to his duchy, in case he should die on so long and dangerous a journey. He had no lawful children, and it was not at all clear who among his kinsfolk had the best right to succeed him. So, after some difficulty, he was able to persuade the wise men of Normandy to accept as their future duke his little son William, who, as his parents had never been married, was called William the Bastard, till he had won a right to be called William the Conqueror and William the Great. William was born before his father became Duke, while he was only Count of the land of Hiesmes, of which Falaise, the town of the rocks, was the capital, where Count Robert had a castle. There is a famous castle there still, but it is somewhat later than William's time, and he certainly was not born in it. But there is no doubt that William was born at Falaise, and that his mother Herleva was the daughter of a tanner of that town, whom Robert afterwards made his chamberlain. Herleva had also a daughter Adelaide by Duke Robert, and after his death she married a knight named Herlwin of

Conteville, to whom she bore two sons, Odo and Robert, William's half-brothers, who play a great part in our story. William was not at all ashamed of the lowliness of his birth on the mother's side, and, when he was duke, he raised her sons to high honour. As he was not Duke Robert's lawful son, he had no right to succeed according to modern law; but the rules of succession were then not at all fixed, and the Normans above all thought but little of lawful marriage and birth in such matters. The chief objection to William's being acknowledged as the future duke was that he was a mere child, about seven years old, so that, if his father died while he was away, he would not be able to govern. But Duke Robert said, " He is little, but he will grow," and at last the wise men of Normandy sware to him. Then Robert went on his pilgrimage and never came back. He died on his way home, in 1035, a long way from his own land, at Nikaia in Asia, where the famous Council of the Church was held in the days of Constantine, and was buried there.

2. **William's Childhood.**—It was after William became duke, but before he was a full-grown man, that the Ætheling Alfred had come to his sad end in England, and that the Ætheling Eadward had been chosen King there. We cannot say how much William had personally to do with either matter. He came to his duchy as a child; but his childhood and youth were of a kind which made him a man, and a strong and wise man, very early. The Norman nobles were very hard to govern at any time, and when the prince was a child, they did whatever they chose. They were always fighting with one another, and sometimes murdering one another by craft. And they were always rebelling against their young duke, and sometimes seeking his life. For it must be remembered that they had not at all wished to have Herleva's son for their lord, and there were several kinsmen of Duke Robert who thought,

and rightly according to our notions, that they had a better right to the duchy than William. The young duke had good and faithful guardians, but several of them were murdered. The land in short was in a state of utter confusion. And now that Normandy was divided and weak, the old friendship with France began to give way, and the French and their kings began again to remember that the settlement of the Normans had cut off France from the sea. So Henry the King of the French joined himself to William's other enemies, and took his castle of Tillières on the French border. Thus he was William's enemy early in his reign, and he became his enemy again afterwards; but in the most dangerous moment of William's Norman reign, the French king was his firm friend. This was in 1047, when a large part of Normandy rose in rebellion against William, of which we must say a little more.

3. **The Revolt of Western Normandy.**—It will be remembered that the western part of Normandy, the lands of Bayeux and Coutances, were won by the Norman dukes after the eastern part, the lands of Rouen and Evreux. And it will be remembered that these western lands, won more lately and fed by new colonies from the North, were still heathen and Danish some while after eastern Normandy had become Christian and French-speaking. Now we may be sure that, long before William's day, all Normandy was Christian, but it is quite possible that the old tongue may have lingered on in the western lands. At any rate there was a wide difference in spirit and feeling between the more French and the more Danish districts, to say nothing of Bayeux, where, before the Normans came, there had been a Saxon settlement. One part of the duchy in short was altogether Romance in speech and manners, while more or less of Teutonic character still clave to the other.

So now Teutonic Normandy rose against Duke William, and Romance Normandy was faithful to him. The nobles of the *Bessin* and *Côtentin* made league with William's cousin Guy of Burgundy, meaning, as far as one can see, to make Guy Duke of Rouen and Evreux, and to have no lord at all for themselves. Their leader was Neal, the Viscount of the Côtentin, the son of the Neal who had beaten back the English invasion in Æthelred's day. When the rebellion broke out, William was among them at Valognes, and they tried to seize him. But his fool warned him in the night; he rode for his life, and got safe to his own Falaise.

4. The Battle of Val-ès-Dunes. — All eastern Normandy was loyal; but William doubted whether he could by himself overcome so strong an array of rebels. So he went to Poissy, between Rouen and Paris, and asked his lord King Henry to help him. So King Henry came with a French army; and the French and those whom we may call the French Normans met the Teutonic Normans in battle at Val-ès-dunes, not very far from Caen. It was William's first pitched battle, a battle of horsemen, in which King and Duke fought hand to hand against the rebels, and each slew some of their chief men. Yet King Henry was once thrown from his horse by a spear from the Côtentin, a deed of which the men of the peninsula sang in their rimes. But they were beaten none the less, and the whole land which had rebelled submitted. Neal escaped, and was after a while pardoned, nor was Duke William's hand at all heavy on his vanquished enemies. But he had vanquished them thoroughly. He was now fully master of his own duchy; and the battle of Val-ès-dunes finally fixed that Normandy should take its character from Romance Rouen and not from Teutonic Bayeux. William had in short overcome Saxons and Danes in Gaul before he came to overcome them in Britain. He had to conquer his own Normandy before he could conquer England, and we shall see that, between these two conquests, he had in some sort to conquer France also.

5. Duke William's Visit to King Edward.—Thus Duke William was for the first time master in Normandy, and four years later it was no doubt said that King Edward was for the first time master in England. Godwine was gone, and the King's Norman favourites had everything their own way. And now the young Duke came to pay his cousin a visit. With so many Normans at the court and in other parts of the land, it might almost seem to him that he was still in his own duchy. Was it now that the thought first came into his head that he might succeed his childless kinsman in a kingdom which looked as if it had already become Norman? Certain it is that William always said that Edward had promised him the crown at his death; and this visit seems a more likely time for such a promise than any time before or after. Of course we must remember that Edward could not, by English law, really leave William the crown; the utmost that he could do would be to recommend the Wise Men to choose him at his death. But just at this time neither William nor Edward was likely to think much about English law, and Edward's Norman counsellors were still less likely to think about it than either of them. We cannot say for certain how it was; but we can hardly doubt that Edward did make William some kind of promise, and this seems the most likely time for it. At any rate William had now conquered Normandy and had visited England. We have to trace two steps towards the time when he again came to England, not as guest but as Conqueror.

6. Duke William in his own Duchy.—We shall see presently that the course of events in England must have altogether thrown back William's hopes with regard to the English crown. But he went on winning fame and power in his own land beyond the sea. He ruled his duchy wisely and well, and it flourished greatly under him. He promoted learned men from other countries, above all two men who lived to play a greater part in England than in Normandy. These were Lanfranc from Pavia in Italy and Anselm from Aosta in Burgundy. They were both monks of the newly-founded monastery of Bec in Normandy, which was at this time a nursery of famous men. The Duke married Matilda, daughter of Baldwin Count of Flanders, by whom he had several daughters and, for the present, three sons, Robert, Richard, and William. The most famous of his daughters was Adela, who married Stephen Count of Blois. But Duke William did not reign without rebellions at home and wars abroad. For a short time after the battle of Val-ès-dunes the friendship between the Duke and King Henry of France went on. Both joined in a war against Geoffrey Count of Anjou, who now held the land of Maine between Anjou and Normandy. In 1049 Duke William for the first time extended his dominions by winning the castles of Domfront and Ambrières in Maine, of which Domfront has ever since been part of Normandy. But before long King Henry got jealous of William's power, and he was now always ready to give help to any Norman rebels. Men in France began again to say that Normandy was a land cut off from France, and that France should be made again to reach to the sea as of old. And the other neighbouring princes were jealous of him as well as the King. His neighbours in Britanny, Anjou, Chartres, and Ponthieu, were all against him. But the great Duke was able to hold his own against them all, and before long to make a great addition to his dominions.

THE YOUTH OF DUKE WILLIAM.

7. Duke William's Wars with France.—The wars between Normandy and France are very important, because they have so great a bearing on English history. There was no quarrel between England and France as long as Normandy lay between them. But France and Normandy had many quarrels and wars; so, when the same prince ruled in England and in Normandy, England was dragged into the quarrels of Normandy, and there grew up a rivalry between England and France which went on after Normandy was conquered by France. These wars therefore between Duke William and King Henry are really the beginning of the long wars between England and France. King Henry invaded Normandy three times. The first time, in 1053, the King came to help a kinsman of the Duke's, William Count of Arques near Dieppe, where the castle with a very deep ditch is still to be seen. This time the French army was caught in an ambush and was utterly routed. In this battle was killed Ingelram Count of Ponthieu, which made room for the accession of his brother Count Guy. The next year, 1054, King Henry came again with a much greater army, gathered from his own kingdom and from the dominions of many of the other princes of Gaul. They came in two great divisions, to attack Normandy on both sides of the Seine. That which came in on the right bank was utterly cut to pieces in the town of Mortemer, which they had occupied and where the Normans attacked them by night. Then the Duke sent a messenger who crossed to the other side of the river where the King's own army was, where he climbed a tree and shouted to them in the darkness to go bury their friends who were dead at Mortemer. So they were seized with a panic and fled. In this battle the new Count of Ponthieu, Guy, was taken prisoner, and was not let go till he became Duke William's man for his county.

Peace was now made with France, and Duke William was allowed to make some conquests at the expense of Anjou. But very soon France and Anjou were again allied against Normandy. In 1058 King Henry made his last invasion. This time the French army was cut off by a sudden attack at the ford of Varaville near the Dive. All these campaigns show that William, who could fight so well in a pitched battle, was no less skilful in all kinds of cunning enterprises. Soon after this, in 1060, both King Henry and Geoffrey of Anjou died. William was now safe from all attacks on that side, all the more so as the new King of the French, Philip, was a child, and the Regent was William's own father-in-law Count Baldwin of Flanders.

8. The Conquest of Maine. — Thus William, who in some sort conquered his own Normandy at Val-ès-dunes, did in some sort also conquer France at Mortemer and Varaville. But he had not yet enlarged his dominions, except at Domfront and Ambrières and one or two other points on the frontier towards Maine. He was presently able to win the whole county. And this part of William's life should be carefully studied, because his conquest of Maine is strikingly like his conquest of England. In both cases he won a land against the will of its people, and yet with some show of legal right. Maine had had counts of its own, some of them famous men, as were also many of the bishops of the great city of Le Mans; the citizens too were stout and jealous of their freedom. But latterly the land of Maine had come under the power of Geoffrey of Anjou. On Geoffrey's death, the lawful Count Herbert, to get back his county, commended himself to William, and they settled that William's son Robert should marry Herbert's sister Margaret, and that Maine should pass to their descendants. This was something like Edward's promise of the English crown to William. In 1063 Herbert died childless, and William claimed the county on behalf of his son, though he and Margaret were not yet married. But the people of Maine chose for their count Walter Count of Mantes, who had married Count Herbert's aunt Biota. He was the son of King Edward's sister Godgifu and brother of Ralph of Hereford. This was like the English people choosing Harold. Then William made war on Maine, and occupied the county bit by bit, till the city surrendered and Walter submitted to him. Soon after this Walter and Biota died; William's enemies said that he poisoned them, which is not in the least likely. But from this time he ruled over Maine as well as over Normandy. We shall see that its brave people revolted more than once against both him and his sons. But the conquest of Maine raised William's power and fame to a higher pitch than it reached at any other time before his conquest of England. And, soon after the conquest of Maine, the affairs of Normandy and England, which have stayed apart ever since William's visit to Edward, begin to be joined together. It is time then to go back and see what had been happening meanwhile in England.

CHAPTER V.

HAROLD EARL AND KING.

1. The Return of Godwine and Harold. — WHEN Duke William paid his visit to King Edward in 1052, Godwine and all his family, save only the Lady Edith, were in banishment, and the Normans were in full power in the land. But before long the English were longing to have Godwine back again. Men soon began to tire of the King's foreign favourites, who, it seemed, could not even defend the land against the Welsh. For the Welsh King Gruffydd came into Herefordshire and smote the Normans who held Richard's Castle. Men sent to ask Godwine to come back; he prayed the King to let him come back, and he got Count Baldwin with whom he was staying and also the King of the French to ask for him; but the King's favourites would not let him hearken. Then, in 1052, Godwine made up his mind to come back without the King's leave, as he knew that no Englishman was likely to fight against him. He therefore set sail from Flanders, and Harold and Leofwine set sail from Dublin. The crews of their ships must have been Irish Danes, which perhaps made Englishmen afraid of them. For, when they landed at Porlock in Somerset, the men of the land withstood them, and Harold and Leofwine beat them in a battle and harried the neighbourhood. But when Godwine came to southern England, no man withstood his coming, but in most parts the folk joined him willingly, saying that they would live and die with him. The King got a fleet against him; but the crews had no heart, and the fleet was scattered before Godwine came. At last Godwine's ships and Harold's met, and they sailed up the Thames together, and came before London on September 14. The citizens then said that what the Earl would they would; the King and his earls brought up an army and another fleet, but the men would not fight against Earl Godwine. Then peace was made; it was agreed that an assembly should be held the next day to settle everything. Then Godwine landed, having come back without shedding of blood. Then fear came on all the Normans who were in and near London, and they fled hither and thither. Specially the Norman Archbishop Robert and Ulf Bishop of Dorchester cut their way out of the city, slaying as they went, and went beyond sea, and never came back to England.

2. **The Restoration of Godwine.**—The next day the assembly met, and voted that Godwine and all his family should be restored to all their goods and honours. It was voted also that all the Normans who had misled the King, especially Archbishop Robert, who was gone already, should be banished. So Godwine and Harold got back their earldoms, and the Lady Edith came back from her monastery; only Swegen did not come back; for he had repented him of his sins and gone barefoot on a pilgrimage to Jerusalem, and had died on the way back, about the time that his father and brothers came home. Of the King's Norman friends some were allowed to stay, and Bishop William of London was allowed to keep his bishopric; but from this time no more Normans got bishoprics or other great offices. And the English Bishop Stigand got the archbishopric of Canterbury instead of Robert. This is a thing to be specially remembered; for it was made a charge

against Stigand, Godwine, Harold, and the whole English nation that Robert had been driven from his archbishopric and Stigand put in his place, without the authority of the Pope, but merely by a vote of the English assembly. The Popes therefore never acknowledged Stigand as lawful archbishop, and though he kept the archbishopric till four years after William's coming, many people in England seem to have been afraid to have any great ecclesiastical ceremony done by him. Bishops commonly went to be consecrated by the Pope, or else by the Archbishop of York. It is easy to see how Duke William was able to turn all this to his own ends.

3. **The Death of Godwine.**—At the Easter-tide of the next year, April 15, 1053, Earl Godwine died. He was seized with a fit while at the King's table, and died three days after. The Normans told strange tales about his death, but that is the simple story in our own Chronicles. Then his son Harold succeeded him as Earl of the West-Saxons, and was the chief ruler of England during the remaining thirteen years of Edward's reign. There is no sign of any dispute between the King and the Earl, though Edward's chief favourite was not Harold, but his younger brother Tostig. The King was allowed to have his Norman friends about him in offices of his court, but not to set them over the kingdom. Bishoprics were given either to Englishmen or to men from Lorraine, that is, we should now say, from Belgium, who could most likely speak both Low-Dutch and French. The King's nephew Ralph and his friend Odda kept their earldoms as long as they lived; but, as earldoms fell vacant, they were given to men of the two great families of Godwine and Leofric. Ælfgar son of Leofric succeeded Harold in East-Anglia. In 1055 Siward of Northumberland died, and his earldom was given to

Tostig the son of Godwine. And when in 1057 the Earls Leofric and Ralph died, the earldoms were parted out again. Ælfgar took his father's earldom of Mercia; only Ralph's earldom of Hereford, which needed specially to be guarded against the Welsh, was added to Harold's earldom. Godwine's son Gyrth succeeded Ælfgar in East-Anglia, and his other son Leofwine got Kent and the other shires round London. Thus the greater part of England was under the rule of the house of Godwine, and what was not remained under the house of Leofric; for when Ælfgar died, his son Edwin succeeded him.

4. **The Scottish and Welsh Wars.**—These later years of Edward's reign, in which Harold was truly the ruler of England, were marked by several stirring events. Thus there was a war with Scotland, where the crown had been more than once disputed between two families. The present king Macbeth had come to the crown after a battle in which Duncan the former king was killed. Duncan was a kinsman of Earl Siward, who therefore wished to restore his son Malcolm. In 1054 Siward entered Scotland, defeated Macbeth, and declared Malcolm king; but the war went on for four years longer, till Macbeth and his son were killed and Malcolm got the whole kingdom. Then there were several wars with the Welsh, under their last great king Gruffydd son of Llywelyn. In 1055 Earl Ælfgar was banished; he then joined Gruffydd in an invasion of Herefordshire. Earl Ralph went out to meet him; but either he only knew the French way of fighting or he liked it best. So he made the English go into battle on horseback, to which they were not used, and they were therefore defeated. Ælfgar and Gruffydd then burned and sacked Hereford; but Earl Harold came and fortified the city afresh. Peace was made with Gruffydd, and Ælfgar got his earldom back again. Gruffydd

presently made war again, but he lost part of his lands at the next peace. He seems to have always kept up his connexion with Ælfgar and his family, and he married Ælfgar's daughter Ealdgyth. At last in 1062 his ravages could no longer be borne, and it was determined to subdue him altogether. The next year Earl Harold waged a great campaign in Wales, in which, the better to fight among the mountains, he made the English take to the Welsh way of fighting, and so made all the Welsh submit. Gruffydd was presently killed by his own people, and Earl Harold gave Wales to two princes, Bleddyn and Rhiwallon, to hold as the King's men. These Welsh and Scottish wars make up nearly all that happened between England and other lands during this time. There was peace with Normandy; but Duke William paid no more visits to his cousin the King. Of a visit which Earl Harold made to him we shall speak presently.

5. **The Succession to the Crown.**—All this time men must have been thinking who should be king whenever King Edward should die. By English law, when the king died, the Wise Men chose the next king. But they chose from the kingly house, and, if the last king left a son of an age to rule, he was almost always chosen. Indeed, if he were actually the son of a king, born after his father was crowned, he had a special right to be chosen. But the crown had never been given to a woman, nor does it seem that the son of a king's daughter had any claim above another man. But it was held that, though the crown could not pass by will, yet some weight ought to belong to the wishes of the late King. Now King Edward had no children, and the only man in the kingly house was his nephew Edward, the son of his elder brother Edmund Ironside. This is he who had been sent away as a child in Cnut's time. He was now living in Hungary, with his

wife and three children, Edgar, Margaret, and Christina. King Edward in 1054 sent for him to come to England, doubtless meaning that he should succeed him. This shows that he had quite given up the thought of being succeeded by his Norman cousin. Edward the Ætheling—that is, the king's son, as son of Edmund Ironside—came to England in 1057; but he sickened and died soon after he landed. His son Edgar was quite a child, and was not a king's son. Moreover he was not born in the land, and he could hardly have been much of an Englishman. Men had therefore to think who should be king if King Edward died before Edgar was grown up. One can fancy that the King might have wished to leave the crown to his nephew Earl Ralph; but, though he was the King's nephew, he was not of the kingly house, and he was not an Englishman. Ralph too died the same year. We can hardly doubt that from this time men began to think whether a time might not come when they should have to choose a king not of the kingly house. From this time Earl Harold seems to hold a special place, and to be spoken of in a special way. His name is joined with the King's name in a way which is not usual, and he is even called *Subregulus* or *Under-king*. All this looks as if the thought of choosing him king whenever Edward should die was already in men's minds.

6. **Earl Harold's Church at Waltham.**—In those days almost every great man, both in England and in Normandy, thought it his duty to make some great gift to the Church, commonly to found or enrich some monastery, to build or rebuild its great church or minster. Many monasteries were founded and churches built at this time in Normandy by Duke William and his barons. And it was the same in England. King Edward's great business was to rebuild and enrich the minster of Saint Peter on the

isle of Thorney in the Thames, which, as standing west from the great church of London, the church of Saint Paul, was known as the *West Minster*. So the Lady Edith, Earl Leofric and his wife Godgifu, Earl Siward, Earl Odda, and many bishops and abbots, were busy at this time building churches and founding monasteries. Earl Godwine is the only great man of the time of whom we hear nothing of the kind. Earl Harold, on the other hand, was as bountiful as any of them, only his bounty went, not to the monks, but to the secular clergy. These were those clergy who were not, like the monks, bound by special vows in their own persons but only by the general law of the Church. They were the parish priests and the canons of cathedral and collegiate churches; only in England several cathedral churches were now served by monks, and more were afterwards. For the monks were much more in fashion just now; Earl Harold however, when he founded a great church, placed in it not monks but secular canons. This was at Waltham in Essex. A church had been founded there in Cnut's days by his banner-bearer Tofig the Proud, who put in it a rood or cross which had been brought from Leodgaresburh (afterwards called Montacute) in Somerset, and which was thought to work wonders. Harold now rebuilt Tofig's church on a greater scale; and, whereas Tofig had founded only two priests, Harold raised the number to twelve, one of whom was Dean, and another *Childmaster*. Earl Harold had through his whole life a special reverence for the Holy Cross of Waltham, and in battle the war-cry of his immediate following was "Holy Cross."

7. **Harold and William.**—The Duke of the Normans and the Earl of the West-Saxons were thus both of them winning fame and power, each of them on his own side of the sea. They were beyond all doubt the foremost men, the

one in England, the other in Gaul. But there was a difference between their positions which arose out of the different political conditions of England and Gaul. Harold was a subject of the King of the English, his chief adviser and minister, the ruler under the King of a great part of the kingdom. But he was still a subject, though a subject who had some hope of being some day chosen king over his own land and people. William could not be called a subject of the King of the French; he was a sovereign prince, ruling his own land, and owing at most an external homage to the king. But he had no chance, as Harold had, of ever becoming a king in his own land; his only chance of becoming a king was by winning, either by force or by craft, the crown of England. Harold and William were therefore rivals. By this time they must have known that they were rivals. But as yet nothing had happened to make any open enmity between them. They could hardly have met face to face; but each must have carefully watched the course of the other. And before long they were to meet face to face; but there are so many stories as to the way in which their meeting came about that it is very hard to say anything at all certain about it. Harold made a journey on the continent in 1058, when he made the pilgrimage to Rome. And it is said that, on his way back, he carefully studied the state of things among the princes of Gaul. At that time William's chief enemies, Henry of France, William of Aquitaine, and Geoffrey of Anjou, were all alive, and it may be that Harold had some schemes of alliance with some of them, in case William should ever put forth any dangerous claims. But of the details of this journey we know nothing. The Norman writers always said that Harold at some time or other took an oath to William, which he broke by accepting the English crown. But they tell the story in so many ways, with so many differences of time, place, and circumstances, that we cannot be certain as to any details. The English writers say nothing about the story; but the fact that they do say nothing about it is the best proof that there is some truth in it. For there are many Norman slanders against Harold which they carefully answer; so we may be sure that, if they could have altogether denied this story, if they could have said that Harold never took any oath to William at all, they would gladly have said so. We may therefore believe that Harold did take some kind of oath to William, which oath William was able to say that Harold had broken. But further than this we can say nothing for certain. All that we can do therefore is to tell the story in that way which, out of the many ways in which it is told, seems the least unlikely.

8. **The Oath of Harold.**—It would seem then that, most likely in the year 1064, after the Welsh war, Harold was sailing in the Channel, most likely with his brother Wulfnoth and his sister Ælfgifu. They were wrecked on the coast of Ponthieu, where Count Guy, according to the cruel custom of the time towards shipwrecked people, shut up Harold in prison, in hopes of getting a ransom. But the Earl contrived to send a message to Guy's lord Duke William, and the Duke at once sent to release him, paying Guy a large ransom. William then took Harold to his court at Rouen and kept him there as his guest in all friendship. Harold even consented, in return doubtless for the kindness which the Duke had shown him, to help William in a war which he was carrying on with the Breton Count Conan, a war in which William and Harold together took the town of Dinan. At some stage of this visit Harold took the oath. It seems most likely that the oath really was simply to marry one of William's daughters, but that the oath was accompanied by an act of homage to William. Such acts of homage were often done in return for any favour, without much being meant by them; and

Harold had just received a great favour from William in his release from Guy's prison. The act might be understood in two ways; but it is plain that William would have a great advantage when he came to claim the crown, from the fact that Harold had in any way become his man. All kinds of other stories, some strange, some quite impossible, are told. Harold is made to promise, not only to secure the crown to William on Edward's death, but to give up the castle of Dover and other places in England to be held by Norman garrisons. And there is one specially famous tale how William tricked Harold into swearing quite unwittingly in an unusually solemn way. He was made, so the story ran, to put his hand on a chest, and it was shown to him afterwards that this chest was full of the relics of saints. And those who tell this story are much shocked at the supposed crime of Harold, but seem to see no harm in the trick played by William. The stories all contradict one another; but they all seem to agree in one thing, namely in making Harold promise to marry a daughter of William. And this promise he certainly did not keep. After all this, Harold went back to England, leaving, as it would seem, his brother Wulfnoth as a hostage for fulfilment of his promise, whatever that promise was.

9. The Revolt of Northumberland.—It will be remembered that Tostig the son of Godwine had been made Earl of the Northumbrians on the death of Siward in 1055. Beside Northumberland, his earldom took in the outlying shires of Northampton and Huntingdon. The Norman tales speak of Harold and Tostig as having been enemies from their boyhood; but there is nothing to make us think that there is any truth in this, and Tostig helped Harold in his Welsh wars. Tostig had also some wars of his own with Malcolm of Scotland, who invaded Northumberland, although he and Tostig were sworn brothers.

Tostig also, like Harold, made the pilgrimage to Rome, and, when he and his people were robbed, he used some very bold language to Pope Nicolas. In his own earldom he had a fierce people to rule, and he ruled them fiercely; beginning with stern justice, he gradually sank into oppression. He seems also to have given offence by staying away from his earldom with the King, with whom he was a great favourite, and handing Northumberland over to the rule of one Copsige. At last, when he had put several of the chief men to death and had laid on a very heavy tax, the whole people revolted. This was in October, 1065. They held an assembly at York, in which they declared Tostig deposed, and chose Morkere the son of Ælfgar to be their earl. Under him Oswulf, a descendant of the old earls, was to rule in Bernicia. They rifled Tostig's hoard; they killed his followers and friends, and marched to Northampton, harrying the land as they went. There Morkere's brother Edwin, the Earl of the Mercians, met them with the men of his earldom and a great body of Welshmen. Thus half England was in revolt. Tostig meanwhile was hunting with the King in Wiltshire. The King was eager to make war on the Northumbrians; but Earl Harold wished to make peace, even at the expense of his brother. The King at last gave him full power to settle matters; so he held an assembly at Oxford, and, as he saw that it was hopeless to try to reconcile Tostig and the Northumbrians, he granted their demands. Peace was made, and the laws of Cnut were renewed; that is to say, it was decreed that Northumberland should be as well ruled as it had been in Cnut's day. Morkere was acknowledged as Earl of the Northumbrians; but Northamptonshire and Huntingdonshire were given to Waltheof the son of Siward. And Oswulf, one of the blood of the old Northumbrian earls, ruled, seemingly under Morkere, in the northern part of the earldom, that which was now beginning to be specially called Northumberland. Tostig was banished and sought shelter in Flanders. By this revolution the house of Leofric became again at least as powerful in England as the house of Godwine, setting aside the personal power of Harold.

10. **The Death of Edward.**— We have now come near to the end of King Edward's reign. All this time he had been building the great church of Saint Peter at Westminster, close by his palace, and he was just able to finish it before he died. The Wise Men came together at Westminster for the Christmas feast of 1065; the King wore his crown as usual; but he fell sick before the hallowing of the new minster, which was done on Innocents' Day. Before the feast was over, on January 5th, 1066, he died, the last King of the male line of Cerdic. Before he died, he uttered some strange words which were taken to be a prophecy, and which were in aftertimes understood of the Conquest of England and of the succession of the kings who followed. But his last act was to recommend the Wise Men to choose Earl Harold as king in his stead. The next day, the feast of the Epiphany, King Edward was buried in his own church of Saint Peter. He had built it specially to be the crowning-place and the burying-place of kings. It was put to both uses within a few days after it was hallowed.

11. **The Election and Coronation of Harold.**—And now the time had come for which men must have been looking so long. King Edward was dead; a new king had to be chosen, and there was no one in the kingly house fit to be chosen. As the Christmas feast was not yet over, the Wise Men were still gathered together at Westminster; so that they could choose at once. It is not clear

whether anybody in England knew anything about Harold's oath to William; if anything was known of it, it must have been held to be of no strength. Nor do we know whether the claims either of William or of Edgar were spoken of or thought of. The thing which is certain is that, as soon as Edward was dead, the assembly met, and, according to the late king's wishes, chose Earl Harold King. The next day he was hallowed to king in the new church of Saint Peter; that is, he was crowned and anointed, and he swore the oath to his people. As men had doubts whether Stigand of Canterbury was a lawful archbishop, the rite was done by Ealdred Archbishop of York. Of this there is no real doubt, though some of the Norman writers say that Harold was crowned by Stigand. That is, they wish to imply that he was not lawfully crowned. For in those days the crowning of a king was not a mere pageant. It was his actual admission to the kingly office, just like the consecration of a bishop. Till he was crowned, he might have, by birth or election, the sole right to become king; but he did not become king till the oil was poured on his head and the crown set upon it. So men might argue that, if the rite was done by an archbishop who had no good right to his see, the coronation would not be valid. All this is worth marking, as showing the feelings of the time. But there is no doubt that Harold came to the crown quite regularly, that he was recommended by Edward on his death-bed, that he was regularly chosen by the assembly, and regularly crowned by Archbishop Ealdred. If things had gone on quietly, Harold would most likely have been the first of a new line of kings. This event in our history is very much like what had happened among the Franks three hundred years before. The last King of the house of the Merwings was deposed, and Pippin, the father of the Emperor Charles the Great, was chosen King in his stead. Only in England there was no need to depose Edward, but merely to choose Harold when he died. And in one very important point the change of the kingly house among the English was quite unlike the same change among the Franks. For the Pope specially approved of the election of Pippin, while the Pope was very far from approving of the election of Harold.

12. **King Harold in Northumberland.**—One of the English Chronicles says that the nine months of the reign of Harold were a time of "little stillness." So it truly was; he was hard at work from the very beginning. At what time Duke William first sent to challenge the crown is not certainly known; but it is not likely to have been very long after Harold's crowning. Of this however we shall best speak in another chapter. But the new king found at once that part of his kingdom was not ready to acknowledge him. This was Northumberland, to the people of which land he had lately shown so much favour by confirming their deposition of his own brother, and their choice of Morkere as their earl. Harold had indeed been crowned by their own archbishop, and their chief men must have acknowledged him along with the rest of the Wise Men; but we should remember that at an assembly in London, though there would be many men present from Wessex, Mercia, and East-Anglia, there could not be many from Northumberland. This would indeed be true of almost every assembly that was held at all; for the three usual places were Winchester, Westminster, and Gloucester, all of them places convenient in turn for different parts of southern England, but none of them convenient for Northumberland. But the change of the kingly house was an act of greater weight than any other, and the Northumbrians might have some kind of ground for saying that the choice had been made

without their consent. How far the brother earls Edwin and Morkere had anything to do with stirring up discontent we cannot tell; but their doings both before and after look like it. Anyhow the Northumbrians refused to acknowledge King Harold. The King now did just as he had done a few months before. He did not think of force; but he went himself to York, taking with him his friend Wulfstan Bishop of Worcester, a most holy man, who was afterwards called Saint Wulfstan. At York he held an assembly, and the speeches of the King and the Bishop persuaded the Northhumbrians to submit without any fighting. And it was most likely at this time, and by way of further pleasing the Northhumbrians, that King Harold married Ealdgyth the sister of Edwin and Morkere and widow of the Welsh King Gruffydd. He thus made it quite impossible that he could marry Duke William's daughter. And the Norman writers do not fail to speak against the marriage on that score, and further to blame him for marrying the widow of a man whom he had killed. Yet Harold had simply overcome Gruffydd in fair warfare, and he had nothing to do with his death, which was the deed of Gruffydd's own people.

13. **The Comet.**—King Harold came back from York to Westminster, and there kept his Easter feast. The usual place was Winchester; but London was now growing in importance, and specially so during these few months of Harold's reign. For he was busy the whole time in making ready for the defence of all southern and eastern England, and for this London was the best head-quarters. He did not appoint any earl of the West-Saxons, but kept Wessex in his own hands, while the south-eastern shires formed the earldoms of his brothers Gyrth and Leofwine. We read much of his good government and good laws, which of course simply means that he went on doing as king as he had done as

earl. For any making of new laws he had no time. But he seems to have given what heed he could to ecclesiastical appointments and reform; for it was specially needful for him to get the clergy on his side. One thing specially marked this Easter assembly. A most brilliant comet was seen, which is recorded by all manner of writers both in England and elsewhere. In those days, when astronomy was little known, men believed that a comet was sent as a sign that some great event was going to happen. So now men gazed at the hairy star, and wondered what would come of it. By this time every one must have known something of the great struggle which was coming. The comet, it was thought, foretold the fall of some great power; but they could not yet tell whether it foretold the fall of Harold or the fall of William.

14. **Summary.**—We have thus seen how, after the death of his father, Harold, as Earl of the West-Saxons, gradually became chief ruler of England, and how the path was opened to him to become king on Edward's death. We have seen how he made some kind of oath to Duke William which might be said to be broken by his accepting the crown. We have seen how he was nevertheless regularly named, chosen, and crowned king, and how he got possession of the whole kingdom. We have now to see what was all this while going on beyond sea, what preparations his rival Duke William was making, and what other dangers were threatening England from other quarters.

CHAPTER VI.

THE TWO HAROLDS.

1. **Tostig's Invasion.**—HAROLD and the English people must have known very well by this time the danger which threatened them from Normandy. They did not perhaps think so much of another danger which threatened them at the same time. Besides Duke William, another foe was arming against them, and, as it turned out, it was this other foe who struck the first blow. It was indeed a time of little stillness when men had to guard against two invasions at once. Or rather it was found to be impossible to guard against both of them. While King Harold was doing all that man could do to make the southern coast of England safe against the Norman, another enemy whom he did not look for came against him in the north. This was the famous King of the Northmen, Harold son of Sigurd, called *Hardrada*, that is *Hard-rede*, the stern in counsel. King Harold of Norway came before Duke William of Normandy. And yet King Harold of Norway was not the first to come. After all it was the south of England which was first invaded, but it was by a much smaller enemy than by either the great king or the great duke. This was no other than the banished Earl Tostig. He seems to have been trying to get help anywhere to put him back in his earldom, even at the cost of a foreign conquest of England. Some say that he had been to Nor-

mandy to stir up Duke William, some that he had been to Norway to stir up King Harold. The accounts are not easy to put together. But it is certain that by May he had got together some ships from somewhere or other, and with them he came to Wight. He then plundered along the south coast; but by this time King Harold of England was getting ready his great fleet and army to withstand Duke William. So King Harold marched to the coast, and Tostig sailed away. He then sailed to Lindesey and plundered there. But the Earls Edwin and Morkere drove him away, and he found shelter in Scotland with King Malcolm.

2. **Harold Hardrada.** — Harold of Norway was the most famous warrior of Northern Europe. His youth had been passed in banishment; so he took service under the Eastern Emperors, who now kept a Scandinavian guard called the Warangians. In that force he did many exploits, specially by helping in the war, when in 1038 the Imperial general George Maniakês won back a large part of Sicily from the Saracens. It is even said that he waged war with the Saracens in Africa, and he then made the pilgrimage to Jerusalem, which he is said to have not done without fighting. And there is a stone at Venice, which was brought from Peiraieus the haven of Athens, on which is graven the name of Harold the Tall, and it has been thought that this records some exploits of Harold Hardrada there. And many strange tales are told of him, of his killing dragons and lions, carrying off princesses, and the like. In short he is one of the great heroes of Northern romance. But there is no doubt that he came back to Scandinavia, that he got the kingdom of Norway which had been held by his forefathers, and waged a long war with Swegen of Denmark. Now at the time of Edward's death and our Harold's election the North was at peace. The

great warrior was perhaps tired of peace; and, either of his own thought or because he was stirred up by Tostig, he began to plan an expedition against England. Whether Tostig had stirred him up or not, it is certain that, when he set out, Tostig joined him, bowed to him and became his man, and helped him in his warfare against his own brother and his own country.

3. **Preparations of Harold of England.**—All the summer of the year 1066 King Harold of England was doing all that man could do to put southern England in a state to withstand any attack from Normandy. If he knew at all that King Harold of Norway was coming, it was still his main business, as he could not be everywhere at once, to defend that part of the kingdom which was under his own immediate rule and which was exposed to the more dangerous enemy. The care of the North he had to leave to its own earls, Edwin and Morkere, who were now his brothers-in-law, and who, of all men in the island, were the most concerned to keep Tostig out of it. King Harold then got together the greatest fleet and army that had ever been seen in England, and with them he kept watching the coasts. This was very hard work to do in those days. For only a small part of his army, called his own *housecarls*, were regular paid soldiers; the greater part were the people of the land, whose duty it was to fight for the land when they were called upon. Such an army was ready enough to come together and fight a battle; but it was hard to keep them for a long time under arms without fighting. And it was also very hard to feed them, for of course they could not be allowed to plunder in their own land. The wonderful thing is that King Harold was able to keep them together so long as from May to September. All that time they were waiting for Duke William, and Duke William never came. Early in

September they could hold out no longer; there was no more to eat, and every man wanted to go home and reap his own field. So the great fleet and army broke up, and the land was left without any special defence. And in the course of the very month in which they broke up, both enemies came. In that very September both King Harold of Norway and Duke William of Normandy landed in England. But King Harold of Norway came the first, and indeed the war with him was over before Duke William crossed the sea.

4. **The Voyage of Harold of Norway.**—Whether then he was stirred up by Tostig or whether he set forth of his own will, King Harold of Norway got him together a mighty fleet, and set sail for England, meaning to win the land and reign there. But men said that he and his friends saw strange dreams and visions on the way which forebode evil to the host. One saw the host of England march to the shore, and before them went a wolf, and a witch-wife rode on the wolf, and she fed the wolf with carcases of men, and, as soon as he had eaten one, she had another ready to give him. It is well to mark these stories, which come out of the old tales and songs of the Northmen, as they show what manner of men they were who now came against England for the last time. The whole story of Harold Hardrada is told in one of the grandest of the old Northern tales, but, when we come to examine it by our own Chronicles, we see that only parts of it can be true. But, notwithstanding the bad omens, the great fleet sailed on, and reached the isles of Shetland and Orkney. These were then a Scandinavian earldom, and its earls, Paul and Erling, joined the Norwegian fleet. It was joined too by other Scandinavian princes from Iceland and Ireland, by King Malcolm of Scotland, and at last, when King Harold of Norway reached

the Tyne, by the English traitor Tostig. Whether by agreement or not, he met the Norwegian fleet with whatever following he had, he became the man of Harold Hardrada, and agreed to go on with him against his brother Harold of England. They sailed along the coast of Yorkshire, as Deira was now beginning to be called; they ravaged Cleveland, and met with no resistance till they reached Scarborough. There the Northmen climbed the hills above the town, and threw down great burning masses of wood to set it on fire. Then they sailed on; the men of Holderness fought against them in vain; they entered the mouth of the Humber; the Northumbrians fled before them, and sailed, as the small ships of those times could, a long way up the country, up the river Wharfe to Tadcaster. So the Norwegian fleet was able to sail up the Ouse towards York without hindrance. They reached Riccall, a place about nine miles from York by land, but much further by the river. There the host disembarked; some were left to guard the ships, while the main body of the army, with Harold Hardrada and Tostig at its head, set forth to march upon York.

5. **The Battle of Fulford.** — It would seem that the two brother earls who ruled on either side of the Humber had taken very little care to defend their coasts; but they were no cowards when actual fighting came. They were now together at York; and when the Northmen came near, they marched out with whatever troops they had, and met Harold of Norway at Fulford, two miles from York, on September 20th, 1066. Events now press so fast on one another that we must remember the days of the week, and the battle of Fulford was fought on Wednesday. Though Fulford is much nearer to York than to Riccall, Harold of Norway got thither before the English earls, and was able to choose his own ground. The battle was fought

on a ridge of ground with the river on one side and a ditch and a marsh on the other. On this side was the weakest part, the right, of the Norwegian army; here Earl Morkere charged, and pressed on for a while. But on the left King Harold of Norway, with his royal banner the *Landwaster* beside him, drove all before him. The English presently fled, and not a few, besides those who were slain with the sword, were hurled into the river and into the ditch. The two earls, with the remnant of their host, found shelter at York.

6. **The Surrender of York.** — York held out only four days, and made terms with the enemy on Sunday. An assembly was held, in which Harold Hardrada was received as king, and it was agreed that the men of Northumberland should follow him against southern England. Hostages for the city were given at once, and hostages for the shire were promised. It is plain that all this was not according to the real wishes of the Northumbrians; but one would think that Edwin and Morkere must have been poor commanders, not to have held out a little longer. The Norwegian army now marched to Stamfordbridge, about eight miles north-east of York, on the river Derwent. Thither the hostages were to be brought. It is not very clear why they went away so far from York, and still further from their ships at Riccall. Perhaps it was because there seems to have been a royal house near at Aldby, of which either Tostig or Harold of Norway may have had a fancy for taking possession at once. Anyhow the mass of the army encamped at Stamfordbridge. There was a wooden bridge there across the Derwent, and the host was scattered on both sides of the river.

7. **The March of King Harold of England.** — The men of York needed only to wait one day longer, and they would not have had to bow to Harold of Norway.

For King Harold of England was on his march; that very Sunday when they surrendered he was in Yorkshire; on Monday morning he was in York itself. When the fleet and army which had guarded the south coast had dispersed, the King rode to London, and there he heard the news of the coming of Harold of Norway. It is said that he was sick at the time; but he bore up as well as he could to get ready his army. And the story ran that King Edward appeared in the night to Abbot Æthelsige of Ramsey, and bade him go to the King and tell him to be of good cheer and go forth and smite the enemies of England. Now this story proves something; for those who put it together could not have looked on Harold as a perjurer or usurper or one undutiful to King Edward, as the Normans said he was. Harold was condemned by the Pope at Rome, and yet Englishmen, even in after times, did not think the worse of him for that. So a tale like this is worth telling. In any case King Harold got ready his army, and pressed on as fast as he could. When he left London, he could not have known of the battle of Fulford; but he would hear the news on the way, and it would make him press on yet faster. On Sunday, September 24th, he reached Tadcaster, and reviewed the fleet in the Wharfe. The next morning he reached York. The whole city received him gladly; but he passed on through the city at once to attack the enemy. The land between York and Stamfordbridge lies so that an army coming from York could get very near to Stamfordbridge without being seen. So we read that King Harold of England and his host came unawares on King Harold of Norway and his host. And then, on that same Monday, was fought the first of the two great battles of this year, the fight of Stamfordbridge.

8. **The Battle of Stamfordbridge.**—The Norwegian story has a grand tale to tell of the battle, which may be

read in many books. But it cannot be true; it must have been made many years after. For it describes the English army as made up chiefly of horsemen and archers, which were just the forces which an English army of that time had not. In after days, when Englishmen had taken to the Norman way of fighting, there were English archers and horsemen, and the story must have been written then. But in those days Englishmen fought on foot; those who rode to the field got down from their horses when the fighting began. The heavy-armed first hurled their javelins, and then they fought with their great axes, or sometimes with swords. The sword was the older weapon; the axe had come in under Cnut. The light-armed had javelins, slings, any weapons they could get; the bow was the rarest of all. But though we cannot believe the Norwegian story, we know something of the battle from our own Chroniclers, and there are bits in one of our Latin writers, Henry of Huntingdon, which are plainly translated from an English song. And that song must have been made at the very time, for only a few days later men had something else to think about besides making songs about Stamfordbridge. In this way we learn that the battle began on the right side of the Derwent, that nearest to York. The English army came unawares on the part of the Northmen who were on that side, who were not in order nor fully armed. They were presently cut to pieces. But meanwhile the main body on the other side had time to form under King Harold of Norway and Earl Tostig, and one valiant Northman kept the bridge against the whole English host. He cut down forty men with his axe; one of the few archers in the English army shot an arrow at him in vain; at last a man went below the bridge and pierced him from below through his harness. Then the English crossed, and the real battle began, the fight of the two Harolds. The fight was long and fearful between two armies equally brave, fighting in much the same way, and each led on by a great captain. But in the end the English won a complete victory. Harold of Norway and Tostig were both killed in the battle, and the great mass of the Norwegian army was cut off. Tostig was known by a mark on his body and was buried at York. And King Harold of England, who had marched into York from Tadcaster on the Monday morning, marched back again to York from Stamfordbridge on the same Monday evening, having overthrown the first of the two enemies who threatened him. So the hostages for all Yorkshire were never given to Harold of Norway.

9. **The Days after the Battle.** — The Norwegian army had been cut off at Stamfordbridge; but the Norwegian fleet was still in the Ouse at Riccall. There were Olaf the son of Harold of Norway and the Earls of Orkney. King Harold of England offered them peace; so they came to York and gave hostages, and sware oaths that they would keep friendship towards England. Some days afterwards the feast of victory was kept at York; and while the King was at the board, a messenger came who had ridden as fast as he could from the south to say that the second enemy was come. Duke William of Normandy had landed in Sussex, and was harrying the land. He had indeed landed three days after the fight of Stamfordbridge, Thursday, September 28th, 1066. We must now go back and see all that he had been doing since the crowning of King Harold of England.

CHAPTER VII.

THE COMING OF DUKE WILLIAM.

1. **Duke William's Claims.** — EVERY one who knew what had happened between William and Harold must have known that after that Duke William would certainly claim the English crown whenever King Edward died. He would most likely have done so, even if Harold had never sworn anything to him; but now that Harold had sworn something, whatever it was, he was yet more sure to press his claims than before. It is worth while to stop and think what William's claim really was. The truth is that he had no real claim whatever; but he was able in a cunning way to put several things together, each of which sounded like a claim. And so, by using one argument to one set of people and another to another, he was able to persuade most men out of England that he was the lawful heir to the English crown, kept out of his right by the wrong-doing of Harold. Each of his claims was really very easy to answer; but each was of a kind which was likely to persuade somebody, and the whole list together sounded like a very strong claim indeed. The real case was this. The people of England had a right to choose whom they would for their King, and they had not chosen William. It was indeed usual to choose out of the one kingly house, and Harold did not belong to that house. But then neither did William. William indeed said that he was Edward's near

kinsman and ought to succeed him. And no doubt in lands where the notion of electing kings was going out of memory, where hereditary succession was coming in, but where the rules of hereditary succession were not yet fully fixed, this claim would have an effect on men's minds. But in truth William had no more claim by inheritance than he had by election. He was indeed Edward's kinsman through Edward's mother Emma; but he was not of the house of the Old-English kings, which alone could give him any preference for the crown above other men. And meanwhile there was young Edgar, a nearer kinsman than William, and who was of the old kingly house. And it is worth noticing that, about a hundred years after, when the notion of hereditary succession had taken root, men began to speak, very often of Harold, and sometimes of William too, as wrongdoers against Edgar. But at the time no one thought of this. And according to modern law King Edward himself would also have been a wrong-doer against Edgar; for by modern law Edgar, the grandson of the elder brother, would come before Edward the younger brother. But most surely no one at the time thought of that either. Then William said that Edward had left him the crown. Now there can be little doubt that Edward had once made him some kind of promise; but a king of the English could not leave his crown to any one; he could at most recommend to the Wise Men, and Edward had recommended Harold. William in short had no kind of right to the crown, whether by birth, bequest, or election. But it was easy for him to talk as if he had; and it was still easier to bring in all manner of other things, which had nothing to do with the matter, but which all helped to make a fair show. Harold was his man who had forsworn himself against him. Harold had done despite to the bones of the Norman saints. These might be Harold's own personal sins, but the English people had nothing to do with them. But William found something to say against the English people also. They had, with Harold's father at their head, murdered the Ætheling Alfred, William's cousin, and his Norman companions. They had, Harold among them, driven out many Normans, among them Archbishop Robert, and had set up a schismatic archbishop in his place. They were an ungodly people, who did not show respect enough to the Pope; he, Duke William, would go and teach them better ways. And, if all other arguments should fail, he could offer lands and honours in England to all who would come and help him to conquer England. William in short could show himself all things to all men, from a pious missionary to a mere robber. But mark that all this care to put himself right in men's eyes shows that we have got out of the days of mere violence. When the English entered Britain, when the Danes entered England, when the Northmen settled in what was to be Normandy, they did not think of putting forth so many good reasons for what they did as Duke William put forth now.

2. **Duke William's Challenge.**—All these arguments sounded very well on the mainland; but no one listened to them in England. Yet it was not for want of hearing them. Duke William heard of Edward's death and of Harold's election and coronation in one message; and before long he sent a challenge to the new King. As we have no exact dates, we cannot tell for certain whether this was before or after Harold's journey to Northumberland; but anyhow it was early in his reign. Nor can we say exactly what were the terms of the message. William of course called on Harold to do whatever he had sworn to do. But, as there are many stories as to what it was that Harold had sworn to do, so there are as many

stories, and indeed more, as to what it was that William now called on him to do. Let him give up the kingdom; let him hold it of William as his lord; let him be earl of half of it under William; let him in any case marry William's daughter; he had at all events promised to do that. Now, if the message came after Harold had married Ealdgyth, this last part must have been mockery. Indeed the whole message must have been sent, not with any hope or thought that Harold would do anything because of it, but simply that William might say that he had given his enemy every chance, and might thus seem to put himself yet more in the right and Harold yet more in the wrong. For it is needless to say that whatever William asked Harold refused. As there are different stories about William's challenge, so there are different stories about Harold's answer. In some accounts he is made to give an answer which covers everything. His oath was not binding, because it was not taken freely. He could not give up his kingdom or hold it of William, for the English people had given him the crown, and none but they could take it from him. And as for marrying William's daughter, he says in one account that the daughter whom he had promised to marry was dead, in another that an English king could not marry a foreign wife without the consent of the Wise Men. He is not made to say that he is married already. So the message may have come before he married Ealdgyth, or it may be that that answer would have seemed to the Normans to be only making bad worse.

3. **Duke William's Councils.**—Nothing was now left to William, if he wished for the English crown, but to try and take it by force. His first business then was to see what help he could get in his own duchy. He first got together a small council of his immediate friends and

kinsfolk; they said that they would help him themselves, but that they could not answer for anybody else. Then he gathered a larger council of all the barons of Normandy at Lillebonne. Here there was great opposition. Many men said that it was no part of their duty to their duke to follow him beyond sea; many also said that the undertaking was rash, and that Normandy was not able to conquer England. And in the end the assembly did not come to any general vote; but William talked over the barons one by one, till they all promised to help him; each would give so many ships and so many men. And when the thing was once blazed abroad, men began to take it up eagerly, and all Normandy was full of zeal for the undertaking. The first thing to be done was to make a fleet; so trees were cut down and ships were built, and all the havens of Normandy were busy with the shipbuilding all the summer.. In the course of August the fleet was ready. All the great men of Normandy had made presents of ships. And by that time men enough to fill them had flocked in both from Normandy and from other lands.

4. **Duke William's Negotiations.**—Everything at this time was as lucky for William as it was unlucky for Harold. Harold had two enemies coming against him at once, and he could not bear up against both. So a few years before, if William had set out on such an undertaking as the conquest of England, he would have left his duchy open to several enemies at once. Just now he had no one to fear. All his old enemies were dead; King Henry of France, Duke William of Aquitaine, and Count Geoffrey of Anjou. We have seen that it is not unlikely that Harold had once thought of alliances with some of these princes, in case William had any designs on England. There was no such chance now. The young King Philip of France was

under the guardianship of William's father-in-law Baldwin of
Flanders. In Anjou there was a civil war. The only neigh-
bour likely to be dangerous was Conan of Britanny. He
died about this time in the Angevin war, and there is a tale
that William contrived to poison his bridle, his gloves, and
his hunting-horn. The strange thing is that it is a Norman
writer who mentions this, and that the Bretons say nothing
about it. But it was not like William to poison any one,
and it is certain that, next to his own subjects, no people
followed him so readily as the Bretons. To the King of
the French William sent an embassy; some even say that
he offered to hold England of him. At any rate he made
things safe on the side of France. And he sent to the young
King Henry of Germany, the son of the Emperor Henry.
Here England had, by the death of the Emperor, really lost a
friend, and not merely the enemy of an enemy. Neither of
these kings gave William any help; but they did all that he
wanted; they did nothing against him, and they did not hinder
their subjects from joining his army. But William's greatest
negotiation of all was with the Pope, Alexander the Second.
He tried to show, not only that Harold was a perjurer and
a sinner against the saints, whom the Pope ought to punish,
but also that his enterprise against England would tend
greatly to the advantage of the Roman Church. Discipline
should be better enforced in England, and the money which
was paid to the Pope, called *Romescot* or *Peterpence*, should
be more carefully paid. And besides all this, there were
men at Rome who could see how much the authority of the
Pope would gain, if it were once allowed that they had the
right to dispose of crowns or to judge between one claimant
of a crown and another. Some of the cardinals said that
the Church ought not to meddle in matters of blood or to
set Christians to fight against one another. But the voice of

these just men was overruled, chiefly by the arguments of Hildebrand the Pope's chief counsellor, who was then Archdeacon of Rome, and who was afterwards himself the great Pope Gregory the Seventh. So Pope Alexander, seemingly without hearing any one on the English side, ruled that Harold was a perjured man, and that the cause of Duke William was righteous. So he gave the Duke a hallowed banner and a ring with a hair of Saint Peter. William was thus able to attack England, her king, and her freedom, as if he had been going forth on a holy war against the enemies of the faith.

5. **The Voyage of Duke William.**—In the course of August all was ready. The fleet was built and manned, and the army was ready to cross into England. The place of meeting was at the mouth of the Dive. The number of ships and of men is very differently told us; but the Norman poet Wace, whose father was there, says that the number of ships was 696. They were only large boats for transport, with a single mast and sail. When they were come together at the Dive, they were kept a whole month waiting for a south wind to carry them to England. It would have been better for England if the south wind had blown at once; for in August King Harold and his army were still ready to meet them; but, as it was, the Normans did not come till the first army was disbanded, and till Harold was busy with the war in the north. At last, though a south wind did not come, a west wind did, and the fleet sailed to Saint Valery at the mouth of the Somme, in Count Guy's land of Ponthieu. They were now much nearer to England than they had been at the Dive; but they still could not cross till Wednesday, September 27, two days after the fight of Stamfordbridge. Then at last the south wind blew, and the fleet crossed in the night. The Duke's own ship, the

Mora, the gift of the Duchess Matilda, sailed first with a huge lantern at its mast to guide them. On Thursday morning the Duke of the Normans and his host landed at Pevensey in Sussex. They landed under the walls of the Roman city of Anderida, which had stood forsaken and empty, ever since it had been stormed by the South-Saxons nearly six hundred years before. There was just now no force in those parts able to hinder the Norman landing. There is a story that, as William landed, his foot slipped, and he fell. But, as he arose with his hands full of English earth, he turned and said that he had taken *seizin* or possession of his kingdom, for that the earth of England was in his hands. Anyhow he took his first possession of English ground at Pevensey, where he left a force. He then, on Friday, September 29th, marched to Hastings, which he made his head-quarters. He there threw up a mound and made a wooden castle. And from this centre he began to harry the land far and wide, in order to make King Harold come the sooner and fight.

6. **The March of King Harold.**—The news of Duke William's landing was, as we have seen, brought to King Harold at York as fast as it could be brought. And King Harold set out on his march southwards as fast as man could set out. With his housecarls and such men of the northern shires as were ready to follow him at once, he set forth for London. Edwin and Morkere were bidden to follow with all speed at the head of the whole force of their earldoms, while the King sent forth to gather the men of his own Wessex and of the earldoms of his brothers Gyrth and Leofwine, to come to the muster at London. Thus the men of all southern and eastern England came in at the King's word; but the main strength of the north never came. Edwin and Morkere kept their

men back, most likely hoping to be able to hold their own earldoms against either Harold or William. Thus King Harold got little help in his second struggle from the land which he had saved in the first. While the troops were coming in, the King went to the church which he had himself built at Waltham, and prayed there. And men said that signs and wonders were wrought at his coming; for that the image on the Holy Cross bowed its head, as if to say, 'It is finished.' So the canons of Waltham feared that harm would come to their King and founder. And two of them followed King Harold's host to the place of battle, that they might in anywise see the end.

7. **Duke William's New Message.** — The host was now ready to set forth for Sussex, all but the men of those shires whose force never came at all. And now another messenger came from Duke William to the King in London. A monk of Fécamp, a great abbey in Normandy near the sea-coast, came and stood before the King of the English on his throne. He bade him come down from it and abide a trial at law between himself and the Duke who claimed the crown by the bequest of Edward, and whose man he had himself become. The King—so the Norman writers say—answered that his oath to William, as being unwilling, was of no force, and that any bequest to William was made of no strength by Edward's later recommendation of himself. This answer, it will be seen, did not go to the root of the matter; but it was answer enough to this particular message. The King then sent his message to Duke William to offer his friendship and rich gifts, if he would go quietly out of the land; but that, if he was bent on fighting, he would meet him in battle on the next Saturday. Then Earl Gyrth gave his brother wise but cruel counsel. He said that, as Harold had anyhow sworn to

William, it was not good that he should meet him in fight. Let him, Gyrth, go against Duke William with the host which had already come together; let the King meanwhile wait for fresh troops, and lay waste all the land between London and the sea, so that, even if the Normans won the fight against Gyrth, they would have nothing to eat, and their duke would be driven to go away. But King Harold said that he would never let his brothers and his people go forth to the fight while he himself shrank from it, and that he would never burn a house or lay waste a field in the land over which he was set to be king. So the King marched from London with his host, and on Friday, October 13th, he reached the hill of Senlac, seven miles inland from the Duke's camp at Hastings, and there waited for the attack of the Normans.

8. **King Harold's Camp.**—The English, as has been already said, were used to fighting on foot. They were stout men to hurl their javelins and to meet the enemy hand to hand with their axes; but they had no horsemen and very few archers. The Normans, on the other hand, were the best horsemen and archers in the world. It was therefore King Harold's plan not to attack the enemy, but to let them attack him; not to meet them in a broad plain fit for horsemen, but to hold a strong place in attacking which the Norman horses would be of less use. So he pitched his camp on a hill which stands out from the main line of hills, and the sides of which are in parts very steep; he fenced it in with a palisade, and with a ditch on the south side where the ground was less steep. The land between Hastings and Senlac was woody, broken, and rolling ground, and the ground at the foot of the hill must then have been a mere marsh. The Normans would therefore have much ado to get to the hill and ride up it,

and, if they got to the top, they would find the English standing there ready to cut them down. So wisely had King Harold chosen his place of fighting; for he knew the land of Sussex well.

9. **The Last Challenge.**—Both King Harold and Duke William sent spies to see what the other was doing. It is said that an English spy came back and said that in the Norman camp were more priests than soldiers. In an earlier time both Normans and English had worn their beards; but now the Normans shaved the whole face like priests, while the English wore only their whiskers on the upper lip. So the spy took the shaven Normans for priests. Then King Harold laughed, and said that they would find these priests right valiant fighting men. One tale tells that King Harold and Earl Gyrth rode out together to spy out the Norman camp, and came back unhurt. And it is also said that now, after the camp was pitched on Senlac, Duke William sent yet a last message and challenge to King Harold. Once more, would Harold give up the kingdom to William, according to his oath? Would he and his brother Gyrth hold the kingdom of William as his men? Lastly, if he declined either of these offers, would he meet William in single combat? The crown should be the prize of the victor, and the blood of their followers on both sides would be spared. But King Harold refused all these offers; for to have accepted any of them, even the single combat, would have been to acknowledge that the war was his personal quarrel with William, and not the quarrel of the people of England whose land William had unjustly invaded. It is plain that Harold had no right to stake the crown on the issue of a single combat. If William killed Harold, that would give William no right to the crown, which it was for the people of England to give

to whom they would. And if Harold killed William, the Norman army was not the least likely to go away quietly; there would have been a battle to fight after all. So King Harold assuredly was right in refusing to stake the fate of England on his own single person. All these stories, it must be remembered, come from the Norman writers; our English Chronicles cut the tale very short. But we may be pretty sure that there is some truth in them, and this story of the challenge seems very likely. Anyhow by Friday evening, every man in each army knew that the great fight for the crown and the freedom of England was to be fought on the morrow.

CHAPTER VIII.

THE GREAT BATTLE.

1. **The Authorities.**—BEFORE we tell the tale of the great fight on Senlac which forms the centre of our whole story, it will be well to stop and think for a while of the sources from which the tale comes. Our own Chroniclers tell us very little; the defeat of the king and people of England was a thing on which they did not love to dwell. We have therefore to get most of the details from Norman sources. Of these there are several, among which four are of special importance. There is the Latin prose account by William, Archdeacon of Poitiers, who was in the Conqueror's army, and the account in Latin verse by Guy, Bishop of Amiens, who wrote very soon after. Both of these were courtiers and flatterers of William; still we may learn a good deal from them. A more honest writer, though not so near to the time, is Master Wace, a canon of Bayeux, whose father crossed with William and was therefore most likely in the battle. Wace wrote the history of the Norman dukes in French rime, called the *Roman de Rou*, and in it he gives a full account of the battle. He had clearly taken great pains to find out all that he could about the fight, and about everybody, on the Norman side at least, who was in it. But more precious than all is the famous Tapestry of Bayeux, which contains the whole history of the Conquest, from Harold's voyage to the end of the battle, wrought in stitchwork. This was made very soon

after the time by order of Bishop Odo for his church at Bayeux. These are the main authorities; from them, and from a sight of the ground, it is not hard to make out the story. And we get incidental pieces of knowledge, such as names of men who were in the battle on the English side, from all manner of sources here and there, among them from the great record called Domesday, of which we shall presently speak.

2. **The March of the Normans.**—The Norman writers tell us that Duke William's army spent the night before the battle, the night of Friday, October 13th, in prayer and shrift, while the English spent it in drinking and singing. And certainly, if our men sang some of the old battle-songs, we shall not think the worse of them. But this is the kind of thing which we often find the writers of the victorious side saying of a defeated army. Anyhow both armies were quite ready for their work early on Saturday morning. The Normans marched from Hastings to the height of Telham, opposite Senlac. There they made ready for the fight; the knights mounted their war-horses and put on their harness. The Duke's hauberk was by some chance turned the wrong way; but his ready wit turned this into a good omen, he said that a Duke was going to be turned into a King. Then he mounted his horse; he looked out at the place where his spies told him that the English King was posted, and he vowed that, where Harold's standard stood, he would, if he won that day's fight, build a minster to Saint Martin of Tours. Then the host set out in three divisions. On the left Count Alan of Britanny commanded the Bretons, Poitevins, and Mansels. Among them was one English traitor, Ralph of Wader or of Norfolk. He was seemingly banished by Edward or Harold, and, as he was of Breton descent by his mother, he

now came back among his mother's people. On the right Roger of Montgomery, one of the most famous lords of Normandy, commanded the French and the mercenaries from all parts. In the midst were the Normans themselves, and in the midst of them was the banner which had come from Rome, borne by a knight of Caux named Toustain (that is, Thurstan) the White. Close by it rode the Duke and his two half-brothers, Bishop Odo of Bayeux and Count Robert of Mortain. The Duke carried round his neck the relics on which Harold had sworn. In each of these three divisions were three sets of soldiers. First went the archers and other light-armed foot, who were to try to put the English into disorder with their arrows and other missiles. Then came the heavy-armed foot, who were to try and break down the palisade, and lastly the horsemen. The archers had no defensive armour; the horsemen and heavy-armed foot had coats of mail and helmets with nose-pieces. The knights had their kite-shaped shields, their long lances carried overhand, and their swords for near fight. The Duke and the Bishop alone carried maces instead of swords. The mace was a most terrible and crushing weapon; Odo, it was said, carried it rather than a sword or lance, because the canons of the Church forbade a priest to shed blood. In this array they had to cross the rolling and marshy ground between the hills of Telham and Senlac.

3. **The Array of the English.** — Meanwhile King Harold marshalled his army on the hill, to defend their strong post against the attack of the Normans. All were on foot; those who had horses made use of them only to carry them to the field, and got down when the time came for actual fighting. So we see in the Tapestry King Harold riding round his host to marshal them and exhort them; then he gets down and takes his place in the

battle on foot. The army was made up of soldiers of two very different kinds. There was the King's personal following, his housecarls, his own thanes, and the picked troops generally, among them the men of London who claimed to be the King's special guards, and the men of Kent who claimed to strike the first blow in the battle. They had armour much the same as that of the Normans, with javelins to hurl first of all, and for the close fight either the sword, the older English weapon, or more commonly the great Danish axe which had been brought in by Cnut. This was wielded with both hands, and was the most fearful of all weapons, if the blow reached its mark; but it left its bearer specially exposed while dealing the blow. The men were ranged as closely together as the space needed for wielding their arms would let them; and, besides the palisade, the front ranks made a kind of inner defence with their shields, called the *shield-wall*. The Norman writers were specially struck with the close array of the English, and they speak of them as standing like trees in a wood. Besides these choice troops, there were also the general levies of the neighbouring lands, who came armed anyhow, with such weapons as they could get, the bow being the rarest of all. These inferior troops were placed to the right, on the least exposed part of the hill, while the King with his choice troops stood ready to meet Duke William himself. The King stood between his two ensigns, the national badge, the dragon of Wessex, and his own Standard, a great flag with the figure of a fighting man wrought on it in gold. Close by the King stood his brothers Gyrth and Leofwine, and his other kinsfolk—among them doubtless his uncle Ælfwig, the Abbot of the New Minster at Winchester, who came to the fight with twelve of his monks. Leofric, Abbot of Peterborough, was also there; but we do not hear of any of the bishops. Whether Earl Waltheof was there is not certain; it is certain that Edwin and Morkere were not.

4. **The Beginning of the Battle.**—By nine in the morning, the Normans had reached the hill of Senlac, and the fight began. But before the real attack was made, a juggler or minstrel in the Norman army, known as *Taillefer*, that is the Cleaver of Iron, asked the Duke's leave to strike the first blow. So he rode out, singing songs of Charlemagne, as the French call the Emperor Charles the Great, and of Roland his paladin. Then he threw his sword up in the air and caught it again; he cut down two Englishmen and then was cut down himself. After this mere bravado came the real work. First came a flight of arrows from each division of the Norman army. Then the heavy-armed foot pressed on, to make their way up the hill and to break down the palisade. But the English hurled their javelins at them as they came up, and cut them down with their axes when they came near enough for hand-strokes. The Normans shouted " God help us ;" the English shouted "God Almighty," and the King's own war-cry of " Holy Cross"—the Holy Cross of Waltham. William's heavy-armed foot pressed on along the whole line, the native Normans having to face King Harold's chosen troops in the centre. The attack was vain; they were beaten back, and they could not break down the palisade. Then the horsemen themselves, the Duke at their head, pressed on up the hill-side. But all was in vain; the English kept their strong ground; the Normans had to fall back; the Bretons on the left actually turned and fled. Then the worse-armed and less disciplined English troops could not withstand the temptation to come down from the hill and chase them. The whole line of the Norman army began to waver, and in many parts

to give way. A tale spread that the Duke was killed. William showed himself to his troops, and with his words, looks, and blows, helped by his brother the Bishop, he brought them back to the fight. The flying Bretons now took heart; they turned, and cut in pieces the English who were chasing them. Thus far the resistance of the English had been thoroughly successful, wherever they had obeyed the King's orders and kept within their defences. But the fault of those who had gone down to follow the enemy had weakened the line of defence, and had shown the Normans the true way of winning the day.

5. **The Second Attack.**—Now came the fiercest struggle of the whole day. The Duke and his immediate following tried to break their way into the English enclosure at the very point where the King stood by his standard with his brothers. The two rivals were near coming face to face. At that moment Earl Gyrth hurled his spear, which missed the Duke, but killed his horse and brought his rider to the ground. William then pressed to the barricade on foot, and slew Gyrth in hand to hand fight. At the same time the King's other brother Earl Leofwine was killed. The Duke mounted another horse, and again pressed on; but the barricade and the shield-wall withstood all attempts. On the right the attack of the French division had been more lucky; the palisade was partly broken down. But the English, with their shields and axes, still kept their ground, and the Normans were still unable to gain the top of the hill or to come near the standard.

6. **The Feigned Flight.**—The battle had now gone on for several hours, and Duke William saw that, unless he quite changed his tactics, he had no hope of overcoming the resistance of the English. They had suffered a great loss in the death of the two earls, and their defences were weakened at some points; but the army, as a whole, held its ground as

G

firmly as ever. William then tried a most dangerous stratagem, his taking to which shows how little hope he now had of gaining the day by any direct attack. He saw that his only way was to bring the English down from the hill, as part of them had already come down. He therefore bade his men feign flight. The Normans obeyed; the whole host seemed to be flying. The irregular levies of the English on the right again broke their line; they ran down the hill, and left the part where its ascent was most easy open to the invaders. The Normans now turned on their pursuers, put most of them to flight, and were able to ride up the part of the hill which was left undefended, seemingly about three o'clock in the afternoon. The English had thus lost the advantage of the ground; they had now, on foot, with only the bulwark of their shields, to withstand the horsemen. This however they still did for some hours longer. But the advantage was now on the Norman side, and the battle changed into a series of single combats. The great object of the Normans was to cut their way to the standard, where King Harold still fought. Many men were killed in the attempt; the resistance of the English grew slacker; but still, when evening was coming on, they still fought on with their King at their head, and a new device of the Duke's was needed to bring the battle to an end.

7. **The End of the Battle.**—This new device was to bid his archers shoot in the air, that their arrows might fall, as he said, like bolts from heaven. They were of course bidden specially to aim at those who fought round the standard. Meanwhile twenty knights bound themselves to lower or bear off the standard itself. The archers shot; the knights pressed on; and one arrow had the deadliest effect of all; it pierced the right eye of King Harold. He sank down by the standard; most of the twenty knights were killed, but four reached the

King while he still breathed, slew him with many wounds, and carried off the two ensigns. It was now evening; but, though the King was dead, the fight still went on. Of the King's own chosen troops it would seem that not a man either fled or was taken prisoner. All died at their posts, save a few wounded men who were cast aside as dead, but found strength to get away on the morrow. But the irregular levies fled, some of them on the horses of the slain men. Yet even in this last moment, they knew how to revenge themselves on their conquerors. The Normans, ignorant of the country, pursued in the dark. The English were thus able to draw them to the dangerous place behind the hill, where not a few Normans were slain. But the Duke himself came back to the hill, pitched his tent there, held his midnight feast, and watched there with his host all night.

8. **The Burial of Harold.**—The next day, Sunday, the Duke went over the field, and saw to the burial of his own men. And the women of the neighbourhood came to beg the bodies of their kinsfolk and friends for burial. They were allowed to take them away to the neighbouring churches. But Duke William declared that, if the body of Harold was found, he, as a perjured man, excommunicated by the Pope, should not have Christian burial. Harold's mother Gytha offered a vast sum—the weight in gold of the body, it was said—to be allowed to bury him at Waltham. But William refused, and bade one of his knights, William Malet by name, to bury him, without Christian rites, but otherwise with honour, under a cairn on the rocks of Hastings. Yet there was a tomb of King Harold at Waltham, and it was always said there that two of the canons, who had followed Harold to the place, asked for his body, that, when they could not tell it for his wounds, they called in the help of a woman named Edith, whom he had loved

before he was King, and that she knew it by a mark. They were then allowed to bury him at Waltham. The truth most likely is that King Harold's body fared very much as we know that Earl Waltheof's body fared ten years later. That is, he was first of all buried on the rocks, but afterwards William, now King, relented and allowed him to be buried in his own church. Anyhow there can be no doubt that Harold died in the battle, as all the writers who lived at the time, both Norman and English, say distinctly. But, as often happens in such cases, there afterwards grew up a tale which said that he was not killed, but only badly wounded, that he was carried off alive, and lived for many years, dying at last as a hermit at Chester. The like is told of Harold's brother Gyrth; but there is no reason to believe either tale.

9. **Effects of the Battle.**—It must be well understood that this great victory did not make Duke William King nor put him in possession of the whole land. He still held only part of Sussex, and the people of the rest of the kingdom showed as yet no mind to submit to him. If England had had a leader left like Harold or Gyrth, William might have had to fight as many battles as Cnut had, and that with much less chance of winning in the end. For a large part of England fought willingly on Cnut's side, while William had no friends in England at all, except a few Norman settlers. William did not call himself King till he was regularly crowned more than two months later, and even then he had real possession only of about a third of the kingdom. It was more than three years before he had full possession of all. Still the great fight on Senlac none the less settled the fate of England. For after that fight William never met with any general resistance. He never had to fight another pitched battle against another wearer or claimant of the English crown. He was thus able to conquer

the land bit by bit. How this came about we shall see in the next chapter. But it is very important not to make either too much or too little of the Battle of Senlac or Hastings. It did not make William either formally King or practically master of the kingdom. But, as things turned out, the result of the battle made it certain that he would become both sooner or later.

CHAPTER IX.

How Duke William became King.

1. The Election of Edgar.—AFTER the great battle, Duke William is said to have expected that all England would at once bow to him. In this hope he was disappointed. For a full month after the battle, no one submitted to him except in the places where he actually showed himself with his army. The general mind of England was to choose another king and to carry on the war under him. But it was hard to know whom to choose. Harold's brothers were dead; his sons were young, and it is not even clear whether they were born in lawful wedlock. Edwin and Morkere had by this time reached London; but no one in southern England was the least likely to choose either of them. The only thing left to do was to choose young Edgar, the last of the old kingly house. The Wise Men in London therefore chose Edgar as king. He did one or two acts of kingly power; but he was never full king, as not being crowned. He would doubtless have been crowned at Christmas, had things turned out otherwise. When he was chosen, Edwin and Morkere withdrew their forces and went back to their own earldoms, taking their sister Ealdgyth, the widow of Harold, with them to Chester. They most likely thought, either that William would be satisfied with occupying the lands which had been held by Harold and his brothers, or else that they would be able to hold their own earldoms against him. By so doing, they destroyed the last chance of England, which was for the whole land to rally faithfully round Edgar. Southern England alone, weakened by the slaughter on Senlac, was quite unable to withstand William.

2. **William's March.**—After the battle William waited five days at Hastings, thinking that men would come in and bow to him. But as none came in, he marched on into Kent. The main strength of that land had been cut off in the battle; resistance was therefore not to be thought of, and one place submitted after another. So did Dover, where was one of the few castles in England, and Canterbury. At this point William's march was checked by sickness; but even then he was able to send messengers to Winchester. That city, the dwelling-place of the widowed Lady Edith, also submitted. He then marched towards London; but he did not cross the Thames; his policy was to win the great city by first occupying the lands all round it. He however defeated a sally of the men of London and burned the suburb of Southwark. He then marched along the right bank of the Thames to Wallingford, where he crossed the river. He then struck eastward to Berkhampstead, meaning to hem in London from the north. After Berkhampstead, he had no need, in this first campaign, to march any further as an enemy.

3. **William's Election and Coronation.**—The men of London were at first eager to carry on the war. But they were weakened by the treason of the Northern earls, and, as William gradually came round to the north of the city, their hearts failed them. The Wise Men and the citizens at last agreed that there was nothing to be done but to submit to William. So the King-elect Edgar gave up his claim, and went with Archbishop Ealdred and the other chief men, and offered William the crown. It is said that

he had some scruple in accepting it while he actually held so small a part of the kingdom; but he could not fail to see how great a gain it would be to him in winning the rest, if he could give himself out as the King of the English, lawfully chosen and crowned. He therefore came to London, and on Christmas-day he was regularly crowned and anointed by Ealdred, as Harold had been on the day of the Epiphany. At his crowning his Norman soldiers kept guard outside the minster. And when the people within were asked whether they would have Duke William for their king, and they shouted, Yea, Yea, the Normans outside thought that some harm was doing to the Duke; so—a strange way of helping him, one would think—they set fire to the houses near the church. Others rushed out of the church to quench the fire, and there was much confusion and damage. Thus the new King's old and new subjects quarrelled on the very day of his crowning, though hardly by any fault of his. Meanwhile a fortress, the first beginning of the famous Tower of London, was rising to keep the city in order. While it was building, the King withdrew to Barking in Essex, not far from London.

4. **The Submission of the Northern Earls.**—While King William was at Barking, most of the chief men of the north of England came and bowed to him, as the chief men of the south had done at Berkhampstead. Edwin and Morkere saw by this time that William had no mind for half a kingdom; so they came and bowed to him, and were restored to their earldoms. Most likely Waltheof did the same. So did Copsige, the former favourite and lieutenant of Tostig, and other men of power in those parts. William received them all graciously. But it would seem that Oswulf did not come. At least it is certain that he gave the new King some offence; for before long, in

February, William deprived him of his earldom and gave it to Copsige.

5. William's Position. — William was now King of the English, as far as a regular election and coronation and the submission of the chief men of the land could make him so. But it must not be thought that he had as yet any real authority over the whole kingdom. He had actual possession of the south-eastern part, from Hampshire to Norfolk. Of the chief cities he held London, Winchester, Canterbury, Norwich, and most likely Oxford. And it would seem that he was acknowledged in part of Herefordshire, where a Norman, Osbern by name, one of the old builders of Richard's Castle, had been sheriff under Edward. But in all northern, western, and north-western England, he was only king so far as that there was no other king. No Norman soldier had been seen anywhere near York, Exeter, Lincoln, or Chester. The submission of the earls carried with it no real obedience on the part of their earldoms. But it suited William's policy, now that he was acknowledged as king, to act in all things as if he had full power everywhere. Thus he restored to Edwin and the rest the lands and offices which he had as yet no means of taking from them. Thus he professed to give the earldom of Oswulf to Copsige. This last story teaches us what the real state of things was. The truth is that Copsige, an enemy of Oswulf's, wished to supplant him. It suited his ends to be able to use William's name, and it suited William to give him authority to do so. But William was not able to give Copsige any real power in Northumberland. Very soon after he had gone thither as the earl appointed by the new king, he was killed by the partisans of Oswulf, who kept the earldom till later in the year he was himself killed by a robber.

6. William's Confiscations and Grants of Land.—
In William's reading of the law, he had himself been, ever since Edward's death, not indeed full king, which he could not be till he was crowned and anointed, but the only person who had a right to become king. Those who had hindered him from taking his crown peaceably, those above all who had fought against him at Senlac, were rebels and traitors. Harold, he held, was no king, but only an usurper; in the legal language of William's reign, he is never called King but only Earl, and all his acts as king are looked on as of no strength. In short, in William's view, as no Englishman had fought for him, as many Englishmen had fought against him, the whole land of the kingdom, except of course Church land, was forfeited to the crown. He might, if he chose, take it all, and either keep it himself or grant it to whom he would. But in the greater part of England he could not as yet do this, and he was too wise to try to do it anywhere all at once. Much land in England, that which was called *folkland*, was in the beginning the common land of the nation. This had been for a long time coming more and more to be looked on as the land of the king. And now that the king was a foreign conqueror, the change was fully carried out, and the *folkland* passed to the new king as his own. So did the great estates of Harold and the rest of the house of Godwine, and of others who had died on Senlac. All this King William took to himself, to keep as the *demesne* of the crown or to reward his Norman followers, as he would. As for the lands of men who submitted quietly, he seems at first to have commonly granted them back again. For this he often took a payment; we read of the English generally buying back their lands, and also of particular cases where this was done. But it was the universal rule that no man, Norman or English, had any right to lands, whether he had

held them before or not, unless he could prove a grant from King William, which was best proved by having the King's writ and seal to show. Thus, from the very beginning of his reign, as any man, Norman or English, offended him or did him good service, William was always seizing on land and making grants of land till, by the end of his reign, by far the greater part of the land of England had changed hands. Most of it was granted to Normans or other strangers, but Englishmen who in any way won his favour both kept their old lands and received new grants. All this began now; but it only began; it was only step by step that the chief offices and estates of England passed from the hands of Englishmen into the hands of strangers. As yet it was only in south-eastern England that he could either take or grant anything.

7. **William's Visit to Normandy.**—King William now thought that it was time to go for a while to his own land; so he crossed into Normandy for the feast of Easter in the year 1067. It was natural that he should wish to show himself to his old friends and subjects in his new character of King and Conqueror. And it was part of his policy too to treat England as if it was thoroughly his own, and thereby to see how far it really was so. In so doing it was needful to provide for the government of the kingdom while he was away. The north he could not help leaving as it was; the part of the kingdom which was really in his power he put under the rule of his brother Bishop Odo and his chief friend William Fitz-Osbern. To them he also gave earldoms, Kent to Odo and Hereford to William. But neither then nor afterwards did he set earls in the old fashion over the whole land; he set them only on the coasts or borders which were likely to be attacked. Thus the Earl of Hereford had to keep the land

against the Welsh, and the Earl of Kent to keep it against any attacks from the mainland. Then the King called on all the chief men of England to go in his train to Normandy. He took with him Edgar the king of a moment, Archbishop Stigand, the Earls Edwin, Morkere, and Waltheof, and other men of power in the land. They all went as his honoured guests and friends, though they were in truth rather to be called hostages and prisoners. He then passed through many parts of Normandy and gave gifts to many churches. He stayed there till December. By that time events had happened which called him back to England.

CHAPTER X.

How King William won the whole Kingdom.

1. The Regency of Bishop Odo and Earl William.— The rule of those whom King William left in England to govern in his name was not of a kind to win much love from the English people. William himself seems to have done all that he could to gain the good will of his new subjects, consistently with firmly establishing his own power. He could be harsh, and even cruel, when it served his purpose; but at no time does he seem to have been guilty of mere wanton oppression for oppression's sake. He was always strict in punishing open wrong-doers of any kind, of whatever nation. It was otherwise with his two lieutenants, Bishop Odo and Earl William Fitz-Osbern. If they did not actually take a pleasure in oppression, they at any rate allowed their followers to do whatever they chose, and, whatever wrong an Englishmen suffered, he could get no redress. Above all things, they everywhere built castles and allowed others to build them, and we have already seen with what horror our forefathers looked on the building of castles. It would almost seem as if oppression was worst immediately under the eyes of the two regents. At least it was in their own earldoms, in Odo's earldom of Kent and in William Fitz-Osbern's earldom of Hereford, that special outbreaks against the new King's authority now broke out. But the two movements were of a different kind. In Kent, which had fully submitted to William, the attempt was strictly a revolt against an established government. In Herefordshire, where the whole land had not submitted, men still tried, just as they might have done before the great battle, to keep the foreign invaders out of a district which they had not yet entered.

2. **Eadric in Herefordshire.**—The chief leader in resistance to the Normans on the Herefordshire border was Eadric, a powerful man in those parts who had never submitted to the new king. He still kept part of the land quite free, holding out in the woods and other difficult places, whence the Normans called him the *Wild* or *Savage*. Earl William's men were always attacking him, but in vain. At last he made an alliance with the Welsh Kings Bleddyn and Rhiwallon, those to whom the kingdom of Gruffydd had been given by Harold. With their help he laid waste the land which had submitted to the Normans, and carried off great plunder. In fact the Normans were never able to overcome Eadric at all, and we shall hear of him again more than once.

3. **Count Eustace at Dover.**—The Kentishmen meanwhile sought for help beyond the sea, as Eadric had sought for help beyond the border; but it was a very strange helper that they chose. They sent to Count Eustace of Boulogne, the brother-in-law of King Edward, the same who had done so much harm at Dover in Edward's days, and who had been one of the four who mangled the dying Harold. They must indeed have been weary of Odo when they sent for Eustace to help them. Why Eustace listened to them is not very clear. William had given him lands in England; we do not hear of any quarrel between them, and Eustace could hardly have thought that he would be able to drive William out and to make himself king instead. However this may be, he sailed across with some troops, and was joined by a large body

of English, chiefly Kentishmen. Their first attempt was on the castle of Dover; but Eustace lost heart and gave way; the garrison sallied; his whole force was routed, and he himself escaped to his own land.

4. **William's Return.**—Besides those who thus openly revolted against William or withstood his power, other Englishmen showed their discontent in various ways. Some left the country altogether; others tried to get help in various parts, above all from King Swegen in Denmark. Swegen, it will be remembered, was nephew of Cnut and cousin of Harold, and there had been talk of choosing him king five-and-twenty years before instead of Edward. If any foreign prince could really have delivered England, Swegen was the man to do it. But he missed the right time when so much of the land was still unsubdued. The worst was that Englishmen could not agree to act together. One district rose at one time and one at another. Some were for Swegen, some for Edgar, some for the sons of Harold; Edwin and Morkere were for themselves. So there was no common action against William, and the land was won bit by bit. In December William came back. He held an assembly at Westminster, where much land was confiscated and granted out again. He also caused Count Eustace to be tried in his absence and outlawed. As Count of Boulogne, Eustace owed William no allegiance; but as his man, holding lands in England, he could be thus tried and outlawed. In after times Eustace gained the King's favour again, and got back his lands. William also sent embassies to various foreign princes, to hinder anything from being done against him in their lands. Especially he sent the English Abbot Æthelsige as ambassador to King Swegen. And he made two appointments which are worth noticing. The bishopric of Dorchester was vacant; so he gave it to a Norman monk, Remigius of Fécamp.

This was the beginning of a system which he carried on through his whole reign, that of giving bishoprics, as they became vacant, to Normans and other foreigners. Also the earldom of Northumberland was vacant by the death of Oswulf. William had not the least authority in Northumberland; yet he made a show of again granting—or rather in truth of selling—the earldom to Gospatric, a man of the kin of the old earls. But Gospatric was as yet no more able to take possession than Copsige had been.

5. **The Siege of Exeter.**— In the spring of 1068 William began seriously to undertake the conquest of that part of England where his kingship was still a mere name. All western, central, and northern England — all Northumberland in the old sense, the greater part of Mercia, and a large part of Wessex—was still unsubdued. At this moment the state of things in the West was specially threatening. Exeter, above all, the greatest city of the West, was the centre of all resistance. Gytha, the widow of Godwine and mother of Harold, was there, most likely with her grandsons, Godwine, Edmund, and Magnus. The citizens of Exeter made leagues with the other towns of the West; men joined them from other parts of England; if the other unconquered districts had risen at the same time, and if they could all have agreed on some one course, it may be that even now William could have been driven out. But while the West was in arms, the North stayed quiet, and even in Exeter itself men were not fully of one mind. Before William went forth to war, he sent a message to the men of Exeter, demanding that they should swear oaths to him and receive him into the city. They sent word that they would pay him the tribute which they had been used to pay to the old kings, but that they would swear no oaths to him nor receive him within their walls. That is, they would be

a separate commonwealth, paying him tribute, but they would not have him as their immediate king. William was not likely to allow this kind of half-submission; so he began his march against Exeter, taking care to call on the force of the shires which were already conquered to come with him. To strike fear into his chief enemy, he took and harried the towns of Dorset on his way. The great men of the city were frightened and sent to William, making submission and giving hostages. But the commons disowned the submission; so William laid siege to the city, after he had put out the eyes of one of the hostages. Exeter held out bravely for eighteen days, and was then taken by undermining one of the towers. William then entered the city, and granted his pardon to the citizens. Gytha and her companions meanwhile escaped by the river. The King then caused a castle called *Rougemont*, or the Red Hill, to be built to keep the city in his power, and he greatly raised the amount of its tribute; but he seems to have done no further harm.

6. **The Conquest of the West.** — The taking of Exeter was followed, at once or before long, by the conquest of all western England. Dorset, Devonshire, Somerset, Cornwall, and most likely Gloucestershire and Worcestershire, were now added to William's dominions. But Eadric still held out in his corner of Herefordshire. William was now master of all Wessex and East-Anglia and of part of Mercia. His conquest of the western lands was clearly followed by many confiscations and grants of land; above all the King's brother Count Robert got nearly all Cornwall, and large estates in other shires. Among these he got the hill in Somerset where the holy cross of Waltham had been found, and which the Normans called *Montacute* or the peaked hill. William now thought

that things were quiet enough for him to bring his wife to England; so at Pentecost, 1068, the Lady Matilda was hallowed to Queen at Westminster by Archbishop Ealdred.

7. **The First Conquest of the North.** — Meanwhile, just after the West was subdued, the North was in arms. Though Edwin, Morkere, and Gospatric were nominally William's earls in Northern England, yet their earldoms had never submitted, and the earls themselves seem to have lived chiefly at William's court. But now all Northern England made ready to resist, York being naturally the centre of the movement, as Exeter had been in the West. They got the Welsh to help them, and sent messages to Scotland and Denmark. The whole land was in arms. And now Earl Gospatric went out and joined his own people, and so did Edgar the Ætheling, and seemingly the Earls Edwin and Morkere also; so there was no lack of leaders. King William marched to meet them as far as Warwick, seemingly his first conquest in this campaign. Near that town the English army met him; but the hearts of Edwin and Morkere failed them. They submitted, and were restored to their earldoms and to William's seeming favour; one of the King's daughters was even promised in marriage to Edwin. The army now dispersed; only a party of the bolder men marched northwards and held Durham. Gospatric, with Edgar and his mother and sisters, found shelter with King Malcolm in Scotland. William had now nothing to do but to march northward, taking one town after another. Some, it would seem, were taken by force, while others submitted peaceably. In all cases he built a castle to keep the town in order; but there was a great difference in his treatment of one town and shire and another. In some parts many more Englishmen kept their lands and offices than in others; these were doubtless those

which submitted most quietly. In this way he occupied most likely Leicester and certainly Nottingham, and so went on to York. The city submitted quietly; but a castle was built. Having thus gained the capital of the North and the main centre of resistance, William did not this time go on any further, but marched back another way, occupying Lincoln, Stamford, Cambridge, and Huntingdon. These two campaigns of the year 1068 gave William a greater part of England than he had won in 1066. Northumberland in the narrower sense with Durham, and north-western Mercia, with Chester as the chief city, were all that now remained unsubdued. But William's hold on some of the lands which had submitted was still very insecure.

8. **The Sons of Harold.** — This same year 1068 the three sons of Harold, Godwine, Edmund, and Magnus, who had escaped with their grandmother Gytha, came back by sea with a force from Ireland, doubtless chiefly Irish Danes. But they did nothing except plunder. They were driven off from Bristol, and then fought a battle with the men of Somerset, who were led by Eadnoth, a man who had been their father's *Staller* or Master of the horse, but who was now in the service of William. Eadnoth was killed, and Harold's sons sailed away, having only made matters worse. Some time in the same year William had a son born to him in England, namely his youngest son Henry. He was the only one of his sons who was born after his father was crowned; so he alone, according to English notions, was a real Ætheling. Moreover he was brought up as an Englishman. He was afterwards King Henry the First.

9. **The First Revolt of York.** — Neither the North nor the West long remained quiet. The year 1069 was still fuller of fighting than the year 1068. But this was

the year in which England was really conquered. At the Christmas feast of 1068 William again made a grant of the earldom of Northumberland in the narrower sense. That land was still quite unsubdued; but now that he had York, it would be easier to attack Durham and the parts beyond. So the King granted the earldom to one Robert of Comines, who set out with a Norman army to take possession. But he fared no better than Copsige had done. The men of the land determined to withstand him; but, through the help of the Bishop Æthelwine, he entered Durham peaceably. But he let his men plunder; so the men of the city and neighbourhood rose and slew him and all his followers. This success encouraged the men of Yorkshire and their leaders who had fled to Scotland. Gospatric and Edgar came back; they were welcomed at York and laid siege to the castle. But King William at once marched north, drove them away, built a second castle, and left his friend Earl William of Hereford in command. He then sent a force against Durham, but it got no further than Northallerton. No sooner was the King gone than the English again attacked the castles at York, but they were defeated by Earl William. And a little later, in June, Harold's sons came again and plundered in Devonshire, but were driven away. So the land was harried alike by friends and by foes.

10. **The Coming of the Danes.**—All this shows how all efforts were in vain, simply for want of a real leader, a king of men like Harold or Edmund Ironside. Englishmen could fight; but their fighting was of no use, when there was no steadiness in the chief men, no concert between one part of the land and another. In fact they seem to have fought best when they had no earls or other great men at their head, when each district fought for itself. In the autumn of this year 1069 there was the best

chance of deliverance of all. A large part of England was in arms at once. The West rose; the men of Somerset and Dorset besieged the new castle of Montacute; the men of Devonshire and Cornwall besieged the new castle of Exeter. On the Welsh border Eadric with a host of Welsh and English attacked Shrewsbury; Staffordshire too, which most likely had not yet submitted, was in arms. But all these movements were put down one by one; save that Staffordshire was left alone for a while. Meanwhile yet greater things were doing in the North. King Swegen of Denmark at last sent a great fleet to the help of the English, under his brother Osbeorn and his sons Harold and Cnut. After some vain attempts on Dover, Sandwich, Ipswich, and Norwich, the Danes entered the Humber, and the English came joyfully to meet them. All the chief men of the north joined them. Edgar and Gospatric came back from Scotland, and this time Earl Waltheof joined them. William's commanders at York, William Malet, he who had first buried Harold's body, and Gilbert of Ghent, sent word to the King that they could hold out for a whole year; but it was not so. The host, Danish and English, began to march on York, and Archbishop Ealdred, worn out with troubles, died as they were coming. The Norman commanders now set fire to the houses near the castles, and a great part of the city was burned. The Danes and English soon reached York; the Normans sallied, and were, some cut to pieces, some made prisoners, the two leaders being among the prisoners. In this fight Earl Waltheof slew many of the enemy, and won himself great fame. The castles were broken down, and York was now quite free from the Normans. But, instead of holding the city, the English dispersed, and the Danes went back to their ships.

11. **The Final Conquest of the North.**—When King William heard of the fall of York, he at once marched

northwards. But when he found that his enemies were all scattered, he left his brother Robert in Lindesey to act against the Danes, while he himself went and subdued Staffordshire, seemingly by hard fighting. He then marched to York, and recovered the city. And now he did one of the most frightful deeds of his life. He caused all northern England, beginning with Yorkshire, to be utterly laid waste, that its people might not be able to fight against him any more. The havoc was fearful; men were starved or sold themselves as slaves, and the land did not recover for many years. Then King William wore his crown and kept his Christmas feast at York. In January 1070 he set out to conquer the extreme north, which was still unsubdued. The Earls Waltheof and Gospatric now craved his pardon. They were restored to their earldoms, and Waltheof received the King's niece Judith in marriage. William then went on to Durham, where the Bishop and nearly everybody had fled from the city, and ravaged the whole land as he had ravaged Yorkshire. He then went back to York by a very hard winter's march, and settled the affairs of his new conquest. He was now at last master of all Northumberland, Deira and Bernicia alike.

12. **End of the Conquest.**—Still William had not yet possession of all England. Not only did Eadric still hold out on his border, and it may be that the Isle of Ely had never fully submitted; but one whole corner of England, and one of the chief cities, still held out. This was Chester. Now then in February 1070 William made another hard winter march from York to Chester. The sufferings of the army were frightful, and many of the mercenaries mutinied. But William went on, and received the submission of the last free English city, whether peaceably or by fighting we know not. He built castles at Chester and Stafford. He then marched to Salis-

bury, where he reviewed and dismissed his army, as having now won the whole land. And so in truth he had. If a few points were still unsubdued, no whole shire or great town held out against him. At last, more than three years after his coronation, he was really king of the whole land in fact as well as in name. From henceforth such opposition to him as we still hear of was no longer resistance to an invader, but rather revolt against an established, though foreign, government.

13. The New Archbishops.—William had now time to turn his mind to the affairs of the Church. Things had naturally got into confusion during the time of warfare; and besides this, William had made up his mind to subdue the Church of England as well as the state, or rather to make the Church a means whereby to hold the kingdom more firmly. As he gradually transferred the greatest estates and highest temporal offices from Englishmen to strangers, so it was part of his policy to do the same with the chief offices of the Church. His rule was that, as the bishops died, Normans or other strangers should be put in their places, and that those of the English bishops against whom any kind of charge could be brought should be deprived without waiting for their deaths. With the abbots the rule was less strict; their temporal position was not so important as that of the bishops. So, though several English abbots were deposed and many foreign abbots were appointed, still a much greater number of Englishmen kept their places than among the bishops, and some Englishmen even received abbeys from William himself. In doing all this he had the help of Pope Alexander and of those who advised him; for it was part of William's policy to strengthen the connexion of England with Rome, though he firmly refused to give up a whit of his own royal power. At the Easter feast of 1070 two papal legates came, and, when the King wore his crown, it was they who put it on his head. A council was then held, in which Archbishop Stigand was deposed, as his right to the archbishopric had all along been thought doubtful. His successor was one of the most famous scholars in Europe. This was Lanfranc of Pavia in Lombardy, who had settled in Normandy and become a monk, and was now abbot of the monastery of Saint Stephen at Caen, which William himself had founded. Lanfranc became Archbishop in August, and was William's right hand man for the rest of his reign. The other archbishopric also was vacant by the death of Ealdred of York. At Pentecost this was given to a Norman, Thomas, a canon of Bayeux, also a great scholar and a careful bishop. For many of William's appointments were very good in themselves, if only the men chosen had not been strangers. These two new archbishops went the next year to Rome to receive from the Pope the pallium or badge of metropolitan dignity; so England had two foreign primates. Stigand's other bishopric of Winchester was also given to another Norman, Walkelin. And so the work went on through the whole of William's reign, till at the end, Saint Wulfstan of Worcester was the only Englishman who was a bishop in England.

14. **The Danes at Ely.**—Before the two foreign archbishops were consecrated, there was again fighting in England. The Danish fleet, which after all had done so little for England, stayed in the Humber while William was subduing Northumberland. William then gave bribes to the Danish commander Osbeorn, and it was agreed that the Danes should sail back when the winter was over, and that, meanwhile they might plunder in England. Thus again was the land harried by friends and foes alike. At last, in May 1070, the Danes sailed to the Fenland, and showed themselves at Ely. The people welcomed them, believing that they would win the land; most likely they were ready

to have Swegen for king. Thus the revolts began almost at the moment when the conquest was finished. We now hear for the first time of the famous name of Hereward. All manner of strange and impossible tales are told of him; but very little is known for certain about him, though what we do know is quite enough to set him before us as a stout champion of England. He had held lands in Lincolnshire, and he had fled away from England, but when or why is not known. He would seem to have come back about the time when the Danes came to Ely, and he joined himself with them and with the men of the land who helped them. The abbey of Peterborough was now vacant by the death of its Abbot Brand, and William had given it to a Norman named Turold. He was a very stern man, and came with a body of Norman soldiers to take possession of the abbey. But Hereward was before him. Lest the wealth of the abbey should be turned to help the enemy, he came (June 1, 1070) with the Danes and the men of the land, and plundered the monastery. The Danes now went away, taking with them much of the spoil of Peterborough. But, when they got home, King Swegen banished his brother Earl Osbeorn for having taken bribes from William and having done so little for England.

15. **The Defence of Ely.**—About this time Eadric the Wild submitted to the King, which marks that all resistance was over on his side of England. But the revolt went on in the Fenland. The monastery of Ely was the centre of resistance, as it stood in a land which then was really an island and which was very easy to defend. The Abbot Thurstan, who had been appointed by King Harold, and his monks, were at first zealous for the patriots. Men flocked to the isle from all parts, and they held out all the winter of 1070 and through the greater part of the next year. In the spring of 1071 the

two earls, Edwin and Morkere, at last left William's court, being, it is said, afraid lest the King should put them in bonds. Edwin tried to get to Scotland, but he was killed on the way, either by his own men or by Normans to whom he was betrayed. But Morkere made his way to Ely and helped in the defence of the isle. Other chief men came also; but it is clear that the soul of the enterprise was Hereward. There are many tales told of his exploits; but this at least is certain. William came and attacked the isle from all points, and there was much fighting for many months, in which William Malet, whom the Danes had released, was killed. At last in October 1071, the isle surrendered. Some say that the monks of Ely, when the King seized their lands outside the isle, turned traitors; others that Morkere and the other chiefs grew fainthearted. Anyhow the war was at an end. The King took possession of the isle; he built a castle at Ely and laid a fine on the abbey, while Morkere and others were kept in prison. Hereward alone did not submit, but sailed out into the sea unconquered. There are several stories of his end. It seems most likely that he was at last received into William's favour, and even served under him in his wars on the mainland. But some say that he was killed by a party of Normans who set upon him without any orders from the King, and that he died fighting bravely, one man against many.

16. **Summary.**—Thus we see that, after five years from William's first landing, he was in full possession of the kingdom and had put down all opposition everywhere. The great battle had given him real possession of south-eastern England only; but it had given him the great advantage of being crowned king before the end of the year. During the year 1067 William made no further conquests; all western and northern England remained unsubdued; but, except in Kent and

Herefordshire, there was no fighting in any part of the land which had really submitted. The next two years were the time in which all England was really conquered. The former part of 1068 gave him the West. The latter part of that year gave him central and northern England as far as Yorkshire, the extreme north and north-west being still unsubdued. The attempt to win Durham in the beginning of 1069 led to two revolts at York. Later in the year all the north and west was again in arms, and the Danish fleet came. But the revolts were put down one by one, and the great winter campaign of 1069-1070 conquered the still unsubdued parts, ending with the taking of Chester. Early in 1070 the whole land was for the first time in William's possession; there was no more fighting, and he was able to give his mind to the more peaceful part of his schemes, what we may call the conquest of the native Church by the appointment of foreign bishops. But in the summer of 1070 began the revolt of the Fenland, and the defence of Ely, which lasted till the autumn of 1071. After that William was full king everywhere without dispute. There was no more national resistance; there was no revolt of any large part of the country. There were still wars within the isle of Britain; but they were wars in which William could give out that he was, as King of the English, fighting for England. And there was one considerable revolt within the kingdom of England; but it was not a revolt of the people. The conquest of the land, as far as fighting goes, was now finished. We have now to see how the land fared under a king who claimed to be king by law, but who had to win his crown by fighting at the head of an invading army. His rule, as we shall see, was neither that of a king who had really succeeded according to law nor yet that of a mere invader who did not even make any pretence to legal right.

CHAPTER XI.

KING WILLIAM'S LATER WARS.

1. The Affairs of Wales.—WILLIAM was now king over all England, but he had not yet won that lordship over the whole of Britain which had been held by the old Kings of the English. But it was his full purpose to win this also, as well as the rule of his immediate kingdom. But of course neither the Scots nor the Welsh were inclined to give him any greater submission than they could help, and there was much fighting on both borders. The care of the Welsh marches William put into the hands of his earls. It was only on the borders and on the exposed coasts that he placed earls at all. Besides his brother Odo in Kent and his friend William Fitz-Osbern at Hereford, there was Earl Gospatric in Northumberland to guard the northern border against the Scots, and Earl Ralph in Norfolk to guard the east coast against the Danes. But he did not appoint any earls to succeed Edwin and Morkere. Parts however of Edwin's earldom were given to two great Norman leaders, Roger of Montgomery who became Earl of Shrewsbury, and Hugh of Avranches who became Earl of Chester. Their duty, along with the Earl of Hereford, was to keep the Welsh march. They received vast estates and special powers, the Earl of Chester especially being more like a vassal prince than an ordinary earl. All these earls had much fighting with the Welsh, and they took much land from them and built many castles. Earl Roger especially built a castle to which he gave the name of his own castle in Normandy, Montgomery, whence a town, and afterwards a shire, took its name. The Welsh princes moreover were always fighting among themselves, and they were often foolish enough to call in the Normans against one another. So the English border advanced. At last in 1081 it is said that King William went on a pilgrimage to Saint David's, and about the same time he founded the castle at Cardiff. Of the three earls of the border, William, Roger, and Hugh, the last two outlived King William. But Earl William Fitz-Osbern left England in 1071, to marry Richildis Countess of Flanders and to try to win her county. There he was killed, and was succeeded in his earldom by his son Roger, of whom we shall hear presently.

2. **The First War with Scotland.**—King Malcolm of Scotland had all this while given himself out as a friend of the English. He had at least promised them help, and he had at any rate given all English exiles a welcome shelter in Scotland. But, as if England had become an enemy's country now that it was conquered by William, in the course of the year 1070 he invaded Northhumberland and harried the land most cruelly, destroying whatever little the Normans had left. Yet none the less, when Edgar and his sisters came to seek shelter again, he received them most kindly, and after a little while he married Edgar's sister Margaret. This marriage was of great importance in the history of Scotland. For Margaret brought English ways into Scotland and made many reforms, and for her goodness she was called a saint. From this time the English part of the dominions of the King of Scots, namely the earldom of Lothian and those parts of Scotland, like Fife, which took to English ways, had altogether the upper

hand over the really Scottish part of the land. No doubt this marriage made William look on Malcolm as still more his enemy, but he could not as yet avenge his inroad. The most part of 1071 he was busy at Ely, and in 1072 he was wanted in Normandy, where the affairs of Flanders made things dangerous. But in August 1072 he set out to invade Scotland by sea and land. It is to be noticed that Eadric, the hero of Herefordshire, went with him. For we can well believe that, now that William was really king over the whole land, Englishmen were quite ready to serve him in a war with the Scots, especially after Malcolm's invasion. But there was no fighting; for Malcolm came and met William at Abernethy and became his man, as, since the days of Edward the Unconquered, the Kings of Scots had ever been to the Kings of the English. Thus had William won, not only the kingdom of all England, but the lordship of all Britain, like the kings who had been before him.

3. **Affairs of Ireland.**—There is in truth some reason to believe that William sought for a lordship even beyond the isle of Britain, such as the kings who were before him had never had. The English Chronicle says that, if King William had lived two years longer, he would have won all Ireland by his wisdom, without any fighting. We cannot tell how this might have been; but it is certain that, though William never had the rule of any part of Ireland, yet in his day England began to have much more to do with Ireland, both with the Danes who were settled there and with the native Irish. This showed itself in bishops from Ireland coming to England to be consecrated by Lanfranc. This was admitting an English supremacy in spiritual things which was very likely to grow into a supremacy in temporal things also.

4. **Affairs of Northumberland.**—As William came back from Scotland, it is to be noticed that he confirmed

the privileges of the bishopric of Durham. He had just given that see to a new bishop, Walcher from Lower Lorraine. The bishops of Durham came gradually to have great temporal rights, like the earls of Chester. Had all earls and all bishops been like these two, the kingdom of England might have fallen to pieces, as Germany did. King William also took away the earldom of Northumberland from Gospatric, and gave it to Waltheof, who was already Earl of Northampton and Huntingdon. Earl Waltheof and Bishop Walcher were close friends. But Waltheof began his rule by a great crime. This was killing the sons of Carl, though they had been his comrades at the taking of York, because their father Carl, a chief man in the North, had killed his own grandfather Ealdred. This was the custom of deadly feud, which was common in Scotland long after. Gospatric went to Scotland, where King Malcolm gave him lands. But he either kept or afterwards received lands in England, and his descendants went on as chief men in the North. One son of his, Dolfin, seems to have received from King Malcolm the little principality of Cumberland in the narrowest sense, that is the land about Carlisle. This was not yet part of the kingdom of England.

5. **The War of Maine.**—William's next warfare was on his own side of the sea. The city and land of Maine, which he had won in 1063, now revolted against him. The men of Maine first chose as their count Hugh the son of the Lombard Marquess Azo, because his mother Gersendis was the sister of their last count Herbert. But she and her husband and son did not agree with the citizens of Le Mans; so the people proclaimed a *commune*. That is, Le Mans should be a free city, as Exeter had striven to be. The whole land of Maine joined the citizens, but they were betrayed by the nobles; so that the story of

Le Mans is like the story of Exeter. Then King William in 1073 crossed the sea, taking with him a great host of English, among whom, there is some reason to think, was Hereward himself. One is sorry to think that a man who had fought so well for freedom in his own land should go and fight against freedom in another land; but we may be sure that the English of that day were glad to fight with French-speaking men anywhere. With this army William laid waste the whole land, and at last the city surrendered, and was, as usual with him, well treated. Le Mans lost its new freedom; but it kept all its old rights and customs. Then William made peace with Count Fulk of Anjou, who also had claims over Maine; William's eldest son Robert was to do homage to Fulk for the county. Thus King William won the land of Maine the second time, ten years after his first conquest.

6. **William's Enemies.**—At this time of his reign William had to spend a great part of his time out of England. King Philip of France was his enemy and Count Robert of Flanders. And Count Robert's daughter was married to Cnut of Denmark, which helped to ally two of his enemies more closely. But the strangest thing is that one German writer says that in 1074 it was fully believed that King William was thinking of an expedition into Germany and of getting himself crowned at Aachen. Another German writer, on the other hand, tells the story quite the other way, and says that King Henry of Germany (who was afterwards Emperor) sent to ask William's help against his own enemies. Either way such stories show that William was very much in men's thoughts and mouths everywhere. And King Philip and Count Robert made a very subtle plot for William's annoyance. This was to plant the Ætheling Edgar at Montreuil, in the land between Normandy and Flanders. He would thus be able to get

together English exiles, men from France and Flanders, and volunteers and mercenaries of all kinds, to trouble the Norman frontier. Edgar was now in Scotland with his sister Queen Margaret. He set out to go to France, but was driven back by a storm. And then William saw that it was his best policy to win Edgar over to himself. So he sent for him to Normandy, and he kept him for many years at his court in great honour.

7. **The Revolt of the Earls.**—Meanwhile a revolt broke out in England, which was not, like the revolt of Ely, a rising of the English people against strangers, but a revolt of a few of the great men for their own ends. Roger, Earl of Hereford, gave his sister Emma in marriage to Ralph, Earl of Norfolk, against the King's orders, which was in itself an offence. Then at the bride-ale they began to talk treason, and to plot how they might kill the King and divide the kingdom. Earl Waltheof too was there; but it is not clear how far he consented to their schemes. On the whole it seems most likely that he at first agreed and swore, and then repented and drew back. He went and confessed to Archbishop Lanfranc, who told him to go and tell the King everything. So Waltheof crossed to Normandy and told everything, and the King received him kindly and kept him with him. Meanwhile the two other earls had revolted openly. But they found few men to help them, except their mercenaries and a number of Bretons who were attached to Earl Ralph. Ralph moreover made a league with King Swegen for a Danish fleet to be sent yet again. The English, who might have risen for Edgar or Swegen, thought that no good was likely to come of a revolt like this, and they fought for the King against the earls. Earl Roger was stopped by Bishop Wulfstan and Abbot Æthelwig; the Norman bishops Odo and Geoffrey went against Earl Ralph, who fled to Denmark,

I

while his wife defended the castle of Norwich against the King. The Danes, under Cnut, came at last, and sailed up to York; but they did nothing except rob the minster. Norwich castle surrendered; the revolt was altogether put down, and those who had a hand in it were punished in various ways; but none of them were put to death.

8. **The Death of Waltheof.** — Ralph of Norfolk had escaped, and his latter end was better than his beginning; for he and his wife went to the crusade and died on the way. Roger of Hereford was kept in prison, some say for the rest of his days. But Waltheof, whose crime, if he had done any, was less than theirs, was in Normandy with the King, and seemingly in his favour. He came back to England with the King, and was soon after put in prison. He was twice brought for trial before an assembly of the great men, and the second time, at Pentecost 1076, he was condemned to death and was beheaded on the hills near Winchester on May 31. This was the only time in his whole reign that William put any man to death except in war. And it is strange that William, who had forgiven his enemies, Waltheof himself among them, over and over again, should have dealt so much more harshly with Waltheof than with Roger and others who were far more guilty. But it is said that Waltheof had many Norman enemies, his wife Judith among them. His earldom of Northumberland was given to his friend Bishop Walcher. The English looked on him as a saint and martyr, and believed that miracles were wrought at his tomb at Crowland. And men generally believed that, after Waltheof's death, King William's good luck, which had hitherto followed him in such a wonderful way, began to forsake him.

9. **The Rebellion of Robert.**—And so it did, whether the death of Waltheof had anything to do with it or not. The very same year the Conqueror suffered his first defeat.

For some reason or other, he besieged Dol in Britanny; but he failed and had to fly. Then his son Robert got discontented, because his father refused to give up any part of his dominions to him. Robert went away, and tried to get various princes to help him. King Philip did give him help, and many of the young nobles of Normandy joined him. In 1079 Philip put him in the castle of Gerberoi, and William came to besiege it. In a sally, Robert overthrew his father, who was saved by the Englishman Tokig, son of Wiggod of Wallingford. But William could not take Gerberoi, and he was persuaded to be reconciled to Robert. Meanwhile Malcolm of Scotland made another frightful inroad into Northumberland, and in 1080 Robert was sent to chastise him. Robert did very little, but on his way back he founded a new castle by the Tyne, whence the town of Newcastle took its name. Robert then again quarrelled with his father, and went away into France, never to come back as long as his father lived.

10. **The Death of Matilda.**—William and his Queen Matilda had lived in all love and confidence up to the time of William's quarrel with Robert. Then for the first time they also quarrelled, because Matilda would send gifts to her son in his banishment, against his father's orders. A little later, in 1083, she died. Their second son Richard had already died in a strange way while hunting in the New Forest, and one of their daughters died while on her way to marry a Spanish king. But, besides Robert, William's other sons, William and Henry, were living; one daughter, Constance, was married to Count Alan of Britanny, and another, Adela, to Count Stephen of Chartres. Another, Cecily, was a nun. Just about the time of Matilda's death there was another revolt in Maine, where the Viscount Hubert held the castle of Sainte-Susanne for three years (1083-1086) against all William's

power. The castle could not be taken, and at last William was driven to receive Hubert to his favour.

11. The Death of Bishop Walcher.—William had thus during these years to undergo several domestic losses and several defeats in war on the mainland. But his hold on England was as firm as ever. After the revolt of the earls, there was nothing which could be called a rebellion, only a local outbreak, in which a local governor lost his life on account of one particular wrong deed. This was Bishop Walcher of Durham, to whom William had given the earldom of Northumberland. This bishop seems, as a temporal ruler, to have been weak rather than oppressive; he is not charged with wrong-doing himself, but with failing to punish wrong-doers. He had several favourites, both English and foreign, who did much mischief. At last some of them murdered one Ligulf, an Englishman of the highest rank in the country, and withal a chief friend of the bishop himself. But even these men he spared, so that the people believed that he had himself a hand in Ligulf's murder. So when an Assembly met to judge the case, the people, headed by the chief Englishmen present, killed the bishop and all his followers. Then Odo was sent to punish them; but he took money, and put innocent men to death, and again harried the land. This was in 1080, the year that Robert was sent against the Scots. This was not a revolt against the Norman king as such, but rather a riot, such as might have happened just as well under Edward or Harold, if any earl of theirs had given the same offence.

12. Death of Cnut of Denmark.—Thus there was nothing, except the inroad of Malcolm, to be called war in England after the revolt of the earls in 1075. But in William's last years a very formidable attack on England was threatened. Cnut of Denmark, who had twice sailed up the Humber, never quite gave up the thoughts of conquering or delivering England. When he himself became king, he made great preparations, and was joined by his father-in-law Robert of Flanders, and by Olaf of Norway, the son of Harold Hardrada. In 1085 Cnut got together a great fleet, and William brought over a vast host of mercenaries to guard the land. But a quarrel arose between Cnut and his brother Olaf, and the next year Cnut was killed in a church by his own men, and was called a saint and martyr. Thus the danger was turned away from William.

13. **Summary.**—We have thus seen how William, having gradually conquered all England, went on to assert the old lordship of the English crown over the rest of Britain. He could not however, any more than the kings before him, keep matters wholly quiet on the Welsh and Scottish borders. In Wales the power of his earls advanced; but King Malcolm, though he became William's man, remained a dangerous enemy. In England there was no real popular revolt after the submission of Ely. The English generally did not favour the rebel earls, and the death of Bishop Walcher was a riot rather than a revolt. On the whole, the land remained quite quiet under William's rule. Beyond sea Maine revolted and was conquered afresh; but after this great success came several petty wars in which William's good fortune came to an end. Yet, when England was concerned, it came back again, as the great preparations of Cnut came to nothing. William had also his domestic troubles, the rebellion of one son, the death of another, and the death of his wife. And in all this the men of the time saw the penalty for the death of Waltheof.

CHAPTER XII.

How King William ruled the Land.

1. William's Government.—We have thus seen how a foreign prince won, and how he kept, the kingdom of England, and how little, after he had once really won it, his rule was disturbed either by revolts at home or by attacks from abroad. We now ask, What was the nature of his government in England all this time? The answer must be that with which we started at first, namely that his government was different both from that of a lawful native king and from that of a conqueror who had come in without any show of right. William was no wanton oppressor, and he no doubt honestly wished to rule his kingdom as well as he could. He even tried to learn English, that he might the better do his duty as an English king. He professed to rule according to the law of King Edward, that is, to rule as well and justly as King Edward had done. And in fact he made very few changes in the old laws; the changes which began with his reign were mostly those gradual changes which could not fail to happen when all circumstances were so greatly changed. The laws might still be the same; but their working could not be the same, when the king was a stranger, and when all the greatest estates and offices had passed into the hands of strangers. By the end of William's reign there were very few Englishmen holding great estates; there was no English earl and only one English bishop. Again, William's government was much stronger than that of any king who had been before him; he was better able to enforce the law, and he did enforce it very strictly. The English writers give him all praise for making good peace in the land, that is for severely punishing all wrong-doers. A king who did this in those days was forgiven much that was bad in other ways. The special complaint which men made against William's government was that he was greedy and covetous, and laid on heavy taxes which men deemed to be wrongful. This is no doubt true; but it is to be remembered that regular taxation was then coming in as something new, and that in no age are men fond of having their money taken from them.

2. **William's Laws.**—William however did make some new laws. These laws were solemnly enacted in the regular assemblies of the kingdom; but then those assemblies were gradually changing from gatherings of Englishmen into gatherings of Normans. He renewed, as the saying went, Edward's Law, with such changes as he said were for the good of the English people. Some of these changes were made merely for the time, while there was still a distinction between English and *French*. This last is the word commonly used to take in both the Normans and all the other French-speaking people whom William had brought with him. Frenchmen who had settled in King Edward's time were to reckon as Englishmen. Normans and Englishmen were to live in peace, but as the Normans were often killed privily, a special law was made for their protection. If the murderer was not to be found, the hundred was to pay. And for some purposes each nation was to keep its own law. Both English and Normans used, in doubtful cases, to appeal to the judgement of God; but the Normans sought to find out

the truth by single combat and the English by the ordeal of hot iron. William allowed both ways, and ordered that each man might keep the custom of his own nation. He forbade the slave-trade by which men were sold out of the land, chiefly to Ireland. This had been forbidden by earlier kings also, but William himself could not wholly get rid of the evil practice. He forbade the punishment of death; criminals might be blinded or mutilated, but not hanged or otherwise killed. This rule he most strictly observed himself, save only in the case of Waltheof. And just at the end of his reign, in 1086, in a great assembly at Salisbury, he made what was in the end the most important law of all. Every man in the land, of whatever other lord he might be the man, swore to be faithful to King William in all things, even against his other lord. Of how great moment this law was we shall see presently.

3. **Changes in the Church.**—Another law of William's had reference to the affairs of the Church. It had hitherto been the custom in England that both civil and ecclesiastical matters should be dealt with in the general assemblies, both of the whole kingdom and of each shire. In these last the earl and the bishop sat together. William now ordered that the bishops should hold separate courts for Church causes. And all through William's reign Lanfranc held many synods of the clergy distinct from the general assemblies of the kingdom. In these synods bishops and abbots were deposed, and many new canons were made. This was the time when Pope Gregory the Seventh was trying to forbid the marriage of the clergy everywhere. In England the secular clergy were very commonly married, both the parish priests and the canons in the secular minsters. The rule which Lanfranc laid down was that no canon should even keep a wife to whom he was already

married; but the parish priests were allowed to keep their wives, only the unmarried were not to marry, nor was any married men to be ordained. Lanfranc was a monk and a favourer of monks; new monasteries were founded, above all King William's abbey of the Battle, built, in discharge of his vow, on the hill of Senlac, with its high altar on the spot where Harold's standard had stood. And monks were put into some churches where there had before been secular priests. The ecclesiastical rule of William and Lanfranc tended on the whole to greater learning and stricter discipline among the clergy; but these gains were purchased by thrusting strangers into all the chief places of the Church as well as of the State.

4. **The New Bishops and Abbots.**—We have said already that, as the bishops and abbots died, or, when there was any pretext for so doing, were deprived, strangers were appointed, always to the bishoprics, commonly to the abbeys. Some of the foreign abbots were rude or fierce men who despised the English. Such was Turold the stern abbot of Peterborough, of whom we have already heard; such was Paul of Saint Alban's, who mocked at the old abbots and pulled down their tombs. Such too was Thurstan of Glastonbury, who, when his monks refused to sing the service after a new fashion, brought soldiers into the church, who slew several of them. But for this King William deposed him. But William's prelates were not as a rule like these. Most of the new bishops worked hard, according to their light, in building their churches, and reforming their chapters and dioceses. Some of them, in obedience to one of Lanfranc's canons, moved their sees from smaller towns to greater. Thus was the see of Lichfield moved to Chester (afterwards to Coventry), that of Elmham to Thetford (afterwards to Norwich), that of Sherborne to Old Salisbury, that of Dorchester

to Lincoln, and, after William's death, that of Wells to Bath. Some of the new prelates lived on good terms with their English neighbours; there is a document in which Saint Wulfstan and his monks of Worcester entered into a bond of spiritual brotherhood with several abbots, Norman and English, and their monks. But besides this, Saint Wulfstan did one good work which was his own. William's law against the slave-trade was at first no better kept than the same law when it was put forth by earlier kings. The men of Bristol still went on selling English slaves to Ireland. Bristol was in Wulfstan's diocese. So he went thither many times, and often preached to the people against their great sin, till they left off sinning, at least for a while.

5. **King William and the Pope.**—While King William helped Lanfranc in all his reforms, he would not give up a whit of the authority in the affairs of the Church which had been held by the kings who had been before him. Both the English kings and the Norman dukes were used to invest bishops and abbots by giving them the ring and staff, the badges of their office. When Hildebrand, who had so greatly favoured William's attack on England, became the famous Pope Gregory the Seventh, he tried with all his might to take away this right from the Emperor and other princes; but to the King of the English he never said a word about the matter, and William himself, and for a while his successors after him, went on investing the prelates just as had been done before. At one time Pope Gregory wrote to the King, demanding that the payment of a penny from each house, called *Romescot* or *Peterpence*, should be more regularly paid, and not only this, but that the King should become his man for his kingdom. To this William wrote back that he would pay the money, because the kings before him had paid it; but that, as no King of the

English before him had ever become the man of the Pope, so neither would he. We must here remark, not only the way in which William stood up for the rights of his crown even against so great a Pope as Gregory, but also the way in which he puts himself exactly in the place of the Old-English kings. Giving himself out as their lawful successor, he claims all that was theirs, but he claims nothing more.

6. **The Imprisonment of Bishop Odo.**—There was another act of William's which shows how fully minded he was that no privilege and no favour should hinder him either from carrying out his own will or from doing whatever he thought was for the good order of his kingdom. His brother Odo, Bishop of Bayeux and Earl of Kent, had got so puffed up with pride and cruelty that he was no longer to be borne. We may believe that the King was specially displeased with his doings in the North when he was sent to punish the riot in which Bishop Walcher was killed. At last, in 1082, Odo fancied that he was going to be made Pope whenever Gregory died, and he got together a great company, or rather an army, in England and Normandy, and was going to set out for Italy. William was then in Normandy; but he came back to England, called an assembly, and formally accused his brother. He said that Odo's misdeeds could no longer be borne; what would the Wise Men of the land counsel him to do? The whole assembly held its peace. Then the King said he must do justice, even against his brother; he bade his barons seize him. But in those days it was thought a great matter to seize a bishop, or indeed any priest. So no man stirred. Then King William seized his brother with his own hands. Odo cried out that it was unlawful to seize a bishop, and that none but the Pope could judge him. It is said that Lanfranc had told the King what to say to this. William answered

that he did not seize the Bishop of Bayeux, but that he did seize the Earl of Kent. So, whatever might become of the Bishop of Bayeux, the Earl of Kent was kept in prison at Rouen. Pope Gregory pleaded earnestly that he might be set free; but William kept him in ward till the day of his own death.

7. The New Forest.—There is no doubt that William was always anxious to do justice, whenever so to do did not hinder his own plans. And this makes a great difference between him and mere oppressors who seem really to like to do mischief. But we have seen that he could do very dreadful things for the sake of his policy, and after a while he came to do things only less dreadful for the sake of his own pleasure. Nearly all men of that time were fond of hunting; William was specially so. For his pleasure in this way he made a forest in Hampshire, not far from his capital at Winchester, and, after eight hundred years, that forest is called the *New Forest* still. It must be remembered that a *forest* does not properly mean land all covered with wood. There were sure to be wooded parts in a forest, but the whole was not wood. A forest is land which is kept waste for hunting, and which is put out of the common law of the land, and ruled by the special and harsher law of the forest. Very hard punishments were decreed against either man or beast that meddled with the king's game. Now, to make or enlarge his New Forest, William did not scruple to turn tilled land into a wilderness, to take men's land from them, and to destroy houses and churches. Just as men thought that William lost his luck after the death of Waltheof, so men thought that the New Forest brought a special curse on his house. Certain it is that three of his house, his two sons Richard and William, and his grandson a son of Robert, all died in a strange way in the Forest.

8. **The Great Survey.**—One of the greatest acts of William's reign, and that by which we come to learn more about England in his time than from any other source, was done in the assembly held at Gloucester at the Christmas of 1085. Then the King had, as the Chronicle says, "very deep speech with his Wise Men." This "deep speech" in English is in French *parlement;* and so we see how our assemblies came by their later name. And the end of the deep speech was that commissioners were sent through all England, save only the bishopric of Durham and the earldom of Northumberland, to make a survey of the land. They were to set down by whom every piece of land, great and small, was held then, by whom it was held in King Edward's day, what it was worth now, and what it had been worth in King Edward's day. All this was written in a book kept at Winchester, which men called *Domesday Book.* It is a most wonderful record, and tells us more of the state of England just at that moment than we know of it for a long time before or after. But above all things we see how far the land had passed from Englishmen to Normans and other strangers. There are only a very few Englishmen who keep great estates at all like those of the chief Normans; but it is quite a mistake to think that every Englishman was driven out of his hearth and home. Crowds of Englishmen keep small estates or fragments of great ones, sometimes held straight of the King, sometimes of a Norman or an Englishman in William's favour. And when any man, Norman or English, had a claim against any other man, Norman or English, it was fairly set down in the book, for the King to judge of.

9. **The Oath of Allegiance.**—Another act, no less important than the great survey, followed close upon it. When the survey was made, and the King knew how all the land in his kingdom was held, he called all the landowners of any

account to a great assembly at Salisbury in August 1086. There they all, of whatever lord they were the men, sware oaths to King William and became his men. That is to say, William had made up his mind to hinder in his kingdom the evils which were growing up in other lands. Elsewhere it was generally held that a man was bound to fight for his own lord, even against his overlord the king. In this way the kingdom of Karolingia or France, and the kingdoms held by the Emperors, broke up into principalities which were practically independent. Most surely William himself would have been greatly amazed if a man of the Duke of the Normans had refused to go against the King of the French. But he took care that there should at least be no such questions in the kingdom of England. Every man in William's kingdom became the King's man first of all, and was to obey him against all other men. There never was any one law made in England of greater moment than this. England for a long time had been getting more united, when the coming of William brought in two sets of tendencies. On the one hand the general strength of his government, and the mere fact that the land was conquered, did much to make the land yet more united. On the other hand, many of William's followers had brought with them the new notions which caused other kingdoms to split in pieces. This wise law settled that the first set of tendencies should get the upper hand, and that the land should become more united by reason of the Conquest. Since William's day no man has ever thought of dividing the kingdom of England.

10. **The Last Tax.**—The great survey and the oath of allegiance were nearly the last acts of William in England. All that he did afterwards was to lay on one more heavy tax. This was a tax of six shillings on every hide of land, a tax which could be both more easily and more fairly raised now

that the survey was made. Men cried out more than ever, and altogether it was a sad and strange time. There were bad crops and fires and famines, and many chief men both in England and Normandy died. And now the time came for the great ruler of both those lands to die also.

CHAPTER XIII.

THE TWO WILLIAMS.

1. **King William's Last War.**—THE way in which the Conqueror came by his death was hardly worthy of the great deeds of his life. The land between Rouen and Paris, on the rivers Seine and Oise, known as the *Vexin*, was a land which had long been disputed between Normandy and France. Border quarrels were always going on, and just now there were great complaints of inroads made by the French commanders in Mantes, the chief town of the Vexin, on the lands of various Normans. William made answer by calling on Philip to give up to him the town of Mantes and the whole Vexin. Philip only answered by making jests on William, who was just now keeping quiet at Rouen, seeking by medical treatment to lessen the bulk of his body. Philip said that the King of the English was lying in, and that there would be a great show of candles at his churching. Then King William was very wroth, and swore his most fearful oaths that, when he rose up, he would light a hundred thousand candles at the cost of the French King. So in August 1087, as soon as he was able to get up, he entered the Vexin and harried the land cruelly. He reached Mantes (August 15), entered the town, caused it to be set on fire, and rode about to see the burning. At last his horse stumbled, perhaps on the burning embers; he was thrown forward on the tall bow of

his saddle, and received a wound inside which made him give over. He was carried to Rouen, and there lay in the priory of Saint Gervase outside the city.

2. **King William's last Sickness.**—He lay there for more than three weeks. The chief prelates of Normandy came about him; some of them were skilful leeches who could tend his body as well as his soul. But they saw that there was no hope, and told him that he must die. He then began to make ready for death. He professed repentance for all his wrong deeds, for the harrying of Northumberland long before and for the burning of Mantes just now. He sent money to make good the destruction at Mantes, and he sent other money to the churches and poor of England. Then he settled the succession to his dominions. He said that by all law Robert must succeed him in Normandy; so it must be; yet he saw what woes would come on the land where Robert should rule. About England he said that he did not dare to make any order; but he wished, if it were God's will, that William should succeed him, and he sent a letter to Archbishop Lanfranc, praying him to crown William, if he thought it right do so. To his youngest son Henry he left five thousand pounds in money from his hoard. Robert was far away, and now his other sons left him, William to look after the kingdom, and Henry to look after his money. Then the King bade all the men, Norman and English, whom he had kept in prison to be set free, save only his brother Odo. Him he said he would not set free; he would only be the cause of more mischief if he were let out. But his brother Robert and others prayed hard 'for him, and at last, much against his will, the King bade that Odo should be set free with the others.

3. **King William's Death and Burial.**—At last on September 9, 1087, the great King William, the Conqueror

of England, died. There was fear and confusion through all Rouen; men knew not what to do, now that the man who had kept the land in peace was gone. For a while the King's body lay stripped and forsaken. But at last he was taken to Caen, to be buried in his own minster of Saint Stephen without the walls. Then, when the rites of burial began, one Asselin the son of Arthur rose and said that the ground on which the church was built was his and his father's, and he forbade that the body should be buried in his soil. So they paid him at once for the grave, and afterwards for the whole estate that he had lost. Then was King William buried, and a shrine of cunning workmanship was made over his grave; but all is now gone.

4. **William the Red.**—The king who was now to succeed William the Great was his third son William—his second son Richard had died in the New Forest. From his ruddy face he was called William Rufus or the Red, and sometimes the Red King. His character was a strange mixture. He had a large share of his father's gifts; he was brave, free of hand, and merry of speech; and, when he chose, he could be both a good captain and a good ruler. But he had none of his father's really great qualities; he was a blasphemer of God and a man of the foulest life; without being so cruel in his own person as some other princes, he was utterly reckless, and cared not how much evil he caused. He was also quite careless of his promises, except when he pledged his word as a good knight; then he kept it faithfully; any one who trusted himself to his personal generosity was always safe. For we have now come to the beginning of what is called chivalry, of which William the Red was one of the first professors. He was proud and self-willed above all men, and he had not, like his father, any steady purpose about any matter. He was

always beginning undertakings and not ending them. Yet there is no doubt that he was a man of great natural gifts, if he had chosen to use them better. He made a great impression on the minds of men at the time, and of no king are there more personal stories told.

5. Accession of William Rufus.—It does not seem that William Rufus was ever regularly chosen king. He crossed to England with his father's letter to Lanfranc, and on September 26, the Archbishop crowned him at Westminster. No one gainsaid his claim; all men bowed to him and sware oaths to him. But it must be remembered that there was really more to be said for either of his brothers than for him. Robert was the eldest son, and was his father's natural successor in Normandy. And those Normans who wished England and Normandy to stay together, would of course wish to have Robert for king in England. On the other hand, if the English had given up all thought of a king of their own blood, the natural choice for them was Henry. He alone was a real Ætheling, a king's son born in the land. But neither Robert nor Henry was at hand, and William took the crown quite quietly. He held the Christmas feast at Westminster, and it seems to have been then that he gave back the earldom of Kent to his uncle Bishop Odo.

6. The Rebellion of Odo.—The new king had been only a few months on the throne, when most of the chief Normans openly rebelled against him, meaning to bring in his brother Duke Robert. At the head of the revolt were the King's two uncles, Count Robert and Bishop Odo. Odo was the first beginner of the whole stir, for he found that he was not, as he had hoped to be, the King's chief counsellor. Earl Roger of Shrewsbury, Bishop Geoffrey of Coutances, Bishop William of Durham, and others of the great men joined them; but Earl Hugh of Chester, Archbishop Lanfranc and all the other bishops, above all Saint Wulfstan at Worcester, remained faithful. Then the King saw that he had nothing to trust to but the native English. So he called them to his standard, and made promises of good government in every way. Then the people flocked to him from all parts, and he found himself at the head of a great English army. The rebels were now smitten everywhere; specially the King with his Englishmen beat back the troops that Duke Robert sent to land at Pevensey. That is, they beat back a new Norman invasion on the very spot where the Conqueror had landed. Then they took the castle of Rochester, where Odo was, and Odo had to come out with shame and to go back to Normandy; he never saw England again. Many of the rebels lost their lands; but they afterwards got them back again when peace was made between King William and his brother Robert.

7. The End of the Conquest.—William Rufus was very far from keeping the promises of good government which he made to the native English when he needed their help. Yet it would be hard to show that he directly oppressed Englishmen as Englishmen; his reign was rather a time of general misrule, which oppressed all classes, though undoubtedly the native English must have suffered the most. But this war of the year 1088 was the last stage of the Norman Conquest. It was the last time that Englishmen and Normans, as such, met in battle against one another on English soil. And, as far as fighting went, the English had the better. In this war Englishmen, fighting against Normans, kept the crown of England for a Norman King. Thus by this war the Norman Conquest of England was in some sort completed and in some sort undone. It was completed so far as that the Norman house was now firmly established on the English throne. From this time no one thought of driving out the kings who came of the line of the Conqueror. No one thought again of setting up Edgar, though he lived a long time after this; no one thought again of asking for help from Denmark. But the Conquest was undone so far as that all this was done by the English themselves, so far as the Norman King was set on the throne by English hands. At this point then we shall best end our tale of the history of the Conquest, and stop to look at the effects which the Conquest had, both at once and on the later history of England.

CHAPTER XIV.

THE RESULTS OF THE NORMAN CONQUEST.

1. General Results of the Conquest. — WE must carefully distinguish the immediate effects of the Norman Conquest, the changes which it made at the moment, from its lasting results which have left their mark on all the times which have come after. In many ways these two have been opposite the one to the other. It might have seemed at the time that the English people had altogether lost their national life, their freedom, their laws, their language, and everything that was theirs. But in truth the Norman Conquest, which at the time seemed to destroy all these things, has actually preserved to us all these things— except our language—more perfectly than we could have kept them if the Norman Conquest had never happened. We can see this by comparing the course of our history with that of other kindred nations which never underwent anything like the Conquest. In no other land have things gone on from the beginning with so little real break as in England. From the earliest times till now, England has never been without a national assembly of some kind. Our national assemblies have changed their name and their form; but they have never wholly stopped; we have never had to begin them again as something altogether new. But in many other lands the national assemblies stopped altogether, and they have had to be set upon as something new in later times, very often after the pattern of ours. And so it is with many other things, which might have died out bit by bit, if there had never been any Conquest, and which might have been suddenly cut short, if the Conquest had been of another kind from what it was. It is the foreign conquest wrought under the guise of law which is the key to everything in English history. And we shall find that the Norman Conquest did not very greatly bring in things which were quite new, but rather strengthened and hastened tendencies which were already at work. We shall see many examples of this as we go on.

2. **Intercourse with other lands.**—One very clear case of this rule is the way in which England now began to have much more to do with other lands than she had had before. But this was only strengthening a tendency which was already at work. From the reign of Æthelred onwards England was beginning to have more and more to do with the mainland. Or rather, whereas England had before had to do, whether in war or in peace, almost wholly with the kindred lands of Scandinavia, Germany, and Flanders, she now began to have much to do with the Latin-speaking people, first in Normandy, then in France itself. The great beginning of this was, as we have already said, the marriage of Æthelred and Emma. Then came the reign of their son Edward, with his foreign ways and foreign favourites. All this in some sort made things ready for the fuller introduction of foreigners and foreign ways at the Conquest. When the same prince reigned over England and Normandy, and when in after times the same prince reigned, not only over England and Normandy, but over other large parts of Gaul, men went backwards and forwards freely from one land to another. If strangers held high offices in England, Englishmen often held high offices in other lands. Our kings too, strangers by descent, went on, even after they had quite become Englishmen, marrying foreign

wives and giving their daughters to foreign princes, far more commonly than had been done before. Foreign trade too increased; England had a very old trade with Germany and Flanders; this in no way ceased, while a great trade with Normandy and other parts of Gaul grew up. And, besides the fighting men and others who followed the kings, not a few merchants and other peaceful men from other lands settled in England. In every way, in short, Britain ceased to be a world of its own; England, and Scotland too, became part of the general world of Western Europe.

3. **Effects of the Conquest on the Church.**—In nothing did this come out more strongly than in the affairs of the Church. The English Church was, more strictly than any other, the child of the Church of Rome, and she had always kept a strong reverence for her parent. But the Church of England had always held a greater independence than the other churches of the West, and the kings and assemblies of the nation had never given up their power in ecclesiastical matters. Church and State were one. But from the time of the Conquest, the Popes got more and more power, as was not wonderful when the Conqueror himself had asked the Pope to judge between him and Harold. Gradually all the new notions spread in England; the Popes encroached more and more, and laws after laws had to be made to restrain them, till the time came when we threw off the Pope's authority altogether. The affairs of Church and State got more and more distinct; the clergy began to claim to be free from all secular jurisdiction and to be tried only in the ecclesiastical courts; the marriage of the clergy too was more and more strictly forbidden. All this was the direct result of the Norman Conquest. If the Conquest had never happened, it might have come about in some other way; but it was in fact

through the Conquest that it did come about. William the Conqueror, like many other great rulers, set up a system which he himself could work, but which smaller men could not work. In after times the kings and popes often played into one another's hands to get their own ends, not uncommonly at the expense of both clergy and people. More than once the whole nation of England, nobles, clergy, and commons, had to rise up against Pope and King together.

4. **Foreign Wars.**—It was also owing to the Norman Conquest that England began to be largely entangled in continental wars. Here again, this might very likely have come about in some other way; but this was the way in which it did come about. As long as Normandy was a separate state lying between England and France, England and France could hardly have any grounds of quarrel. But when England and Normandy had one prince, England got entangled in the quarrels between Normandy and France. England and France became rival powers, and the rivalry went on for ages after Normandy had been conquered by France. Then too both England and Normandy passed to princes who had other great possessions in Gaul, and the chief of these, the duchy of Aquitaine, was kept by the English kings long after the loss of Normandy. Thus, through the Norman Conquest, England became a continental power, mixed up with continental wars and politics, and above all, engaged in a long rivalry with France.

5. **Effects on the Kingly Power.** — One chief result of the Norman Conquest was greatly to strengthen the power of the kings. The Norman kings kept all the powers, rights, and revenues which the English kings had had, and they added some new ones. A king may be looked on in two ways. He may either be looked on as the head of the state, of which other men are members, or else as the chief lord, with the chief men of

the land for his men, holding their lands of him. Both these notions of kingship were known in Europe; both were known in England; but William the Conqueror knew how to use both to the strengthening of the kingly power. Where the king is merely the lord of the chief men, the kingdom is likely to split up into separate principalities, as happened both in Germany and in Gaul. William took care that this should not happen in England by making his great law which made every man the man of the king. But when this point was once secured, it added greatly to the king's power that he should be personal lord as well as chief of the state, and that all men should hold their lands of him. The Norman kings were thus able to levy the old taxes as heads of the state, and also to raise money in various ways off the lands which were held of them. They could, like the old kings, call the whole nation to war, and they could further call on the men who held lands of them either to do military service in their own persons or to pay money to be let off. Thus the king could have at pleasure either a national army, or a *feudal* army, that is an army of men who did military service for their *fiefs*, or lastly an army of hired mercenaries. And the kings made use of all three as suited them. Another thing also happened. In the older notion, kingship was an office, the highest office, an office bestowed by the nation, though commonly bestowed on the descendants of former kings. But now kingship came to be looked on more and more as a possession, and it was deemed that it ought to pass, like any other possession, according to the strict rules of inheritance. Thus the crown became more and more hereditary and less and less elective. For several reigns after the Norman Conquest, things so turned out that strict hereditary succession could not be observed. Still, from the time of the Conquest, the tendency was in favour of strict hereditary succession, and it became the rule in the long run.

6. **Effects on the Constitution and Administration.**—We have already seen that both William the Conqueror and the Norman kings after him made very few direct changes in the law. Nor did they make many formal changes in government and administration. They destroyed no old institutions or offices, but they set up some new ones by the side of the old. And of these sometimes the old lived on till later times, and sometimes the new. And sometimes old things got new names, which might make us think that more change happened than really did. And in this case again sometimes the old names lived on and sometimes the new. Thus the Normans called the *shire* the *county*, and the king's chief officer in it, the *sheriff*, they called the *viscount*. Now we use the word *county* oftener than the word *shire;* but the sheriff is never called *viscount*, a word which has got another meaning. So, in the greatest case of all, the King is still called *King* by his Old-English name, but the assembly of the nation, the *Witenagemót* or Meeting of the Wise Men, is called a *Parliament*. But this is simply because the wise men spoke or *parleyed* with the king, as we read before that King William had "very deep speech with his Wise Men" before he ordered the great survey. What is much more important than the change of name is that the assembly has quite changed its constitution. And yet it is truly the same assembly going on; there has been no sudden break; changes have been made bit by bit; but we have never been without a national assembly of some kind, and there never was any time when one kind of assembly was abolished and another kind put in its stead. The greatest change that ever happened in a short time was that, in the twenty-one years of the

Conqueror's reign, an assembly which was almost wholly an assembly of Englishmen changed into one which was almost wholly an assembly of Normans. But even this change was not made all at once. There was no time when Englishmen as a body were turned out, and Normans as a body put in. Only, as the Englishmen who held great offices died or lost them one by one, Normans and other strangers were put in their places one by one. Thus there came a great change in the spirit and working of the assembly; but there was little or no immediate change in its form. And so it was in every thing else. Without any sudden change, without ever abolishing old things and setting up new ones, new ideas came in and practically made great changes in things which were hardly at all changed in form. It is a mistake to think that our Old-English institutions were ever abolished and new Norman institutions set up in their stead. But it is quite true that our Old-English institutions were greatly changed, bit by bit, by new ways of thinking and doing brought over from Normandy.

7. **Effects of the Conqueror's Personal Character.**—Besides all other more general causes, there can be no doubt that the personal character of William himself had a great effect on the whole later course of English history. As William had no love for oppression for its own sake, so neither had he any love for change for its own sake. He saw that, without making any violent changes in English law, he could get to himself as much power as he could wish for. Both he and the kings for some time after him were practically despots, kings, that is, who did according to their own will. But they did according to their own will, because they kept on all the old forms of freedom; so, in after times, as the kings grew weaker and the nation grew stronger, life could be put again into the forms, and the old freedom could be won back again. A smaller

man than William, one less strong and wise, would most likely have changed a great deal more. And by so doing he would have raised far more opposition, and would have done far more mischief in the long run. ⟨William's whole position was that he was lawful King of the English, reigning according to English law.⟩ But a smaller man than William would hardly have been able at once outwardly to keep that position, and at the same time really to do in all things as he thought fit. It is largely owing to William's wisdom that there was no violent change, no sudden break, but that the general system of things went on as before, allowing this and that to be changed bit by bit in after times, as change was found to be needed.

8. **Relations of Normans and Englishmen.** — It followed almost necessarily from the peculiar nature of William's conquest that in no conquest did the conquerors and the conquered sooner join together into one people. No doubt the fact that Normans and English were after all kindred nations had something to do with this; but the union could hardly have been made so speedily and so thoroughly, if it had not been for the peculiar character of the conquest made under the form of law. William took a great deal of land from Englishmen and gave it to Normans; but every Norman to whom he gave land had in some sort to become an Englishman in order to hold it. He held it from the King of the English according to the law of England; he stepped exactly into the place of the Englishman who had held the land before him; he took his rights, his powers, his burthens, whatever they might be, neither more nor less. He had to obey and to administer English law, to hold English offices, to adapt himself in endless ways to the customs of the land in which he found himself. And, except in the case of the very greatest nobles, there were men of Old-

English birth by his side, holding their lands as he held his, holding offices, attending in assemblies, acting with him in every way as members of the same political body. The son of the Norman settler, born in the land, often the son of an English mother, soon came to feel himself more English than Norman. So the two nations were soon mingled together, so soon that a writer a hundred years after the Conquest could say that, among freemen, it was impossible to say who was English and who was Norman by descent. Of course in thus mixing together, the two nations influenced one another; each learned and borrowed something from the other. The English did not become Normans; the Normans did become Englishmen; but the Normans, in becoming Englishmen, greatly influenced the English nation, and brought in many ways of thinking and doing which had not been known in England before.

9. **Effects of the Conquest on Language.**—Above all things, this took place in the matter of language. In this we carry about us to this day the most speaking signs of the Norman Conquest. If the Norman Conquest had never happened, the English tongue would doubtless have greatly changed in the course of eight hundred years, just as the other tongues of Europe have greatly changed in that time. But it could not have changed in the same way or the same degree. No other European tongue has changed in exactly the same way, because no other tongue has had the same causes of change brought to bear on it. Our own Old-English tongue, as it was spoken when the Normans came, was a pure Teutonic tongue, that is, it was as nearly pure as any tongue ever is; for there is no tongue which has not borrowed some words from others. So we had, since we came into Britain, picked up a few words from the Welsh, and more from the Latin. But these

were simply names of things which we knew nothing about till we came hither, foreign things which we called by foreign names. And we had kept our grammar, and what grammarians call the *inflexions*, that is, the forms and endings of words, quite untouched. The Normans, on the other hand, after their settlement in Gaul, had quite forgotten their old Danish tongue, allied to the English, and, when they came to England, they all spoke French. French is the *Romance* tongue of Northern Gaul, that is, the tongue which grew up there as the Latin tongue lost its old form, and a good many Teutonic words crept in. The effect of the Norman Conquest on our tongue has been twofold. We have lost nearly all our inflexions; we should very likely have lost most of them if there had been no Norman Conquest, for the other Teutonic tongues have all lost some or all of their inflexions; but the Norman Conquest made this work begin sooner and go on quicker. Then we borrowed a vast number of French words, many of them words which we did not want at all, names of things which already had English names. But this happened very gradually. For some while the two languages, French and English, were spoken side by side without greatly affecting one another. French was the polite speech, Latin the learned speech, English the speech of the people; but for a hundred and fifty years after the Conquest, French was never used in public documents. Before long the Normans in England learned to speak English, and they seem to have done so commonly by the end of the twelfth century, though of course they could speak French as well. Then there came in a French, as distinguished from a Norman influence; French came in as a fashion, and it was not till the fourteenth century that English quite won the day; and when it came in, it had lost many of its inflexions, and borrowed very many French words. And since this we have gone on taking in new words from French, Latin, and other tongues, because we have lost the habit of making new words in our own tongue. All these later changes are not direct effects of the Norman Conquest; still they are effects. The French fashion could never have set in so strongly if the French tongue had not been already brought in by the Normans.

10. **Effects of the Conquest on Learning and Literature.**—There can be no doubt that in all matters of learning the Norman Conquest caused a great immediate advance in England. There had in earlier times been more than one learned period in England; but the Danish wars had thrown things back, and it does not seem that Edward, with all his love for strangers, did much to encourage foreign scholars. But with the coming of William this changed at once. Lanfranc and Anselm for instance, the first archbishops of Canterbury after the Conquest, were the greatest scholars of their time. Men of learning and science of all kinds came to England, and men in England, both of Norman and of English blood, took to learning and science. We have therefore during the twelfth century a large stock of good writers who were born or who lived in England. But they wrote in Latin, as was usual then and long after with learned men throughout western Europe; they therefore did nothing for the encouragement of a native literature. Still men did not leave off writing in English; the English Chronicle goes on during the first half of the twelfth century, and small pieces, chiefly religious, were still written. But the Norman Conquest had the effect of thrusting down English literature into a lower place; even when it was commonly spoken, it ceased to be either a learned or a polite tongue. On the other hand, the newly-born French literature took great root in England. It was about the time of the Conquest

that men in Northern Gaul found out that the French tongue which they talked had become so different from the Latin which they wrote that it would be possible to write in French as well as to speak it. The oldest French books, like the oldest books of most languages, are in verse, and this new French verse flourished greatly among the Normans, both in Normandy and in England. Thus Wace wrote the story of the Norman dukes, and specially of the Conquest of England. Others, who were settled in England and began to love their new land, wrote books of English and British history and legend. Thus, for a long time after the Conquest, there was much writing going on in England in all three languages. Many French writings were translated into English, and some English writings into French. But all this, though it showed how men's minds were at work, kept down the real tongue and the real literature of the land for several ages.

11. **Effects of the Conquest on Art.**—In those days there was not much art in Western Europe, save the art of building. Books were illuminated, and there was both painting and sculpture in churches, but they were what would be now thought very rude work. Both in Germany and in England the art of embroidery seems to have flourished; but that is hardly art in any high sense. But in the art of building the Norman Conquest of England marks a great stage. When we speak of building, we have mainly to do with churches and castles; houses were commonly of wood, as indeed churches and castles often were also. In the eleventh century men still built throughout Christendom with round arches, after the manner of the old Romans. And in Western Europe they built everywhere very much after the same pattern, one which came from Italy. But in the eleventh century men began to strike out new ways in architecture, and, without wholly for-

saking the old Roman models with their round arches, they devised new local styles in different parts. Thus one form of what is called *Romanesque* architecture arose in Italy, another in Southern Gaul, another in Northern Gaul, and so on. The Normans of William's day were great builders, and the Romanesque style of Northern Gaul grew up chiefly in Normandy, and is commonly called *Norman*. In Edward's day this new style came into England among other Norman fashions, and under William it took firmer root. The new prelates despised the English churches as too small, and they rebuilt them on a greater scale, and of course in the new style. For a while the old style which England had in common with the rest of Western Europe was still used in smaller buildings; but by the end of the eleventh century the Norman style had taken full root in England, and in the twelfth century it grew much richer and lighter. And as stone building came more and more into use, the style spread to houses and other buildings.

12. **Effects of the Conquest on Warfare.**—Military architecture, the building of castles and other strong places, is in some sort a part of the history of the building art, no less than the building of churches and houses. Still it has a character and a history of its own. In this matter, and in all matters which had to do with warfare, the Norman Conquest made the greatest change of all. In England men could fence in a town with walls, but they had no strong castles. Their strong places were great mounds with a wooden defence on the top. But the Normans brought in the fashion of building castles, as we have seen in the history of Edward's reign. They sometimes built lighter keeps on the old mounds; sometimes they built massive strong towers; and in either case they were fond of surrounding them with deep ditches. These were the

types which the Normans brought in, and they grew into the elaborate castles of later times. Thus the land was filled with castles, and warfare took mainly the form of attacking and besieging them. After the Norman Conquest we hear for a long time much more of sieges, and much less of battles in the open field, while in the Danish wars we heard much more of battles than of sieges. The Normans also brought their own way of fighting into England, and made great changes in English armies. Before the Conquest we had no horsemen and very few archers; from this time we have both, and the old array goes out of use. Yet we sometimes read of the Norman knights getting down from their horses and fighting with swords or axes in Old-English fashion. And, as the archers came to be the strongest part of an English army, and that which was thought specially English, it was in one way a going back to the old state of things. The weapon was changed; but, in times when horsemen were most thought of, a stout body of foot was still the strength of an English army.

13. **Summary.**—Thus we see the special way in which the Norman Conquest, owing to its own special nature and to the personal character of William, acted upon England. It did not destroy or abolish our old laws or institutions; but by influencing, it gradually changed, and in the end preserved. And in this way the Conquest worked in the end for good. We have really kept a more direct connexion with the oldest times, without any sudden break or change, than those kindred nations which have never in the same way been conquered by strangers. There has been great change, but it has been all bit by bit, with no general upsetting at any particular time. We will now, in our last chapter, see a little more particularly how these causes worked in the later history of England.

CHAPTER XV.

THE LATER HISTORY.

1. The Norman Kings.—WILLIAM RUFUS began his reign as a Norman king of England only; Robert held the duchy of Normandy. But William got, first part and then the whole, of Normandy into his hands, and he afterwards warred with France. Here then is the beginning of our French wars, wars which the French writers from the very beginning speak of as wars of the English against the French. William Rufus' reign was one of great oppression and wrong, and in his time, under his minister Randolf Flambard, the new customs about the holding of land got put into a definite shape. At his death in 1100 Normandy and England were again separated for a while, for Robert again took his duchy, while Henry was chosen King of the English. As he was the only one of the Conqueror's children who was in any sense English, the native English were strongly for him, and helped him to keep the crown, when the Normans again wished for Robert. This is the last time that we hear of the English and Normans in England acting as separate classes of people. The reign of Henry, which lasted till 1135, was the time in which the two races were gradually joined together. Henry also pleased the English by marrying Edith or Matilda, the daughter of Malcolm King of Scots and Margaret the sister of the Ætheling Edgar. Thus his children sprang in the female line from the old kings. Then Robert ruled Normandy so ill that many of his own people wished to get rid of him; so in 1106 King Henry won the duchy at the battle of Tinchebrai. This was just forty years after William the Great had won England, and men began to say that things were now turned round. Henry's son, William the Ætheling, died before him. He therefore wished his crown to go to his daughter Matilda, the widow of the Emperor Henry the Fifth, whom he married to Count Geoffrey of Anjou. For the rule to pass to a woman was a strange thing both in England and in Normandy. So when Henry died, men chose his sister's son Stephen of Blois. Stephen was much loved by men of all races, but he had not strength to reign in those times. The friends of the Empress rose up against him, and through the whole of Stephen's days, till 1154, there was such a time as England never saw before or since. All law vanished, and there was nothing but bloodshed and plunder. Meanwhile Count Geoffrey conquered Normandy. At last it was settled that Stephen should keep the crown for life, but that the son of Geoffrey and Matilda, Henry, now Duke of the Normans, should reign after him.

2. **Henry of Anjou.** — Duke Henry soon succeeded Stephen, and with him a new time began. He inherited Normandy and Anjou; he took England by the agreement with Stephen; and before he became king he had married Eleanor, Countess of Poitou and Duchess of Aquitaine, who brought with her all south-western Gaul. Thus the King of the English became a great prince on the mainland, and was far more powerful in Gaul than his lord the King of the French. Normandy and England alike became parts of a vast dominion, the ruler of which was in no way either Norman or English except by female descent. Yet, as he was English by female descent, men

tried to see in him a representative of the old kings. In this state of things all the natives of England, of whatever race, began to draw closer together, and still more so under Henry's sons, when a fashion set in of favouring men who were altogether strangers, neither English nor Norman. This reign was the time of the famous Archbishop Thomas, son of Gilbert Becket. He was born of Norman parents in England in Henry the First's reign, and he was the first man born in the land who became archbishop after the Conquest. We are most concerned with him here, because he shows how the two races were now joined together. Thomas throughout feels and speaks as an Englishman, and everybody looks on him as such. Henry the Second was one of our greatest kings, the first since the Conquest who was really a lawgiver. A great deal of our later law dates from his time, and it is all law made for an united nation, without distinction of Normans and English. It is not clear whether Henry himself spoke English; but he certainly understood it, and it was commonly spoken by men of both races in his time. Henry also increased the greatness of his kingdom by establishing a fuller supremacy over Scotland and by beginning the conquest of Ireland.

3. **The Sons of Henry.**—After Henry in 1189 came his son Richard. He was born in England, but he was really the least English of all our kings. He was only twice in England during his reign, both times for a very little while. He first came to be crowned, and afterwards in 1194 he came to take his crown again. For he went to the crusade, and on his way back he was kept in prison by the Emperor Henry the Sixth. To him he did homage for something, as Harold did to William, and some say that it was for the crown of England that he did homage. The rest of his reign he was chiefly fighting in Gaul; but while

he was away, England was ruled by his ministers. His first chief minister was his chancellor William Longchamp, Bishop of Ely. He came from Normandy, and he despised and mocked Englishmen in every way. But the name of Englishman now took in all men born in the land, and we find another bishop, also born in Normandy, speaking of it as a strange and shameful thing that Bishop William could speak no English. So the nation, under the King's brother Earl John, rose and drove out the foreign chancellor. In the later part of Richard's reign the land was better ruled by his minister Archbishop Hubert. On Richard's death in 1199 Earl John succeeded quietly in Normandy, and was then elected King in England. But in Anjou the notion of hereditary right had taken deeper root, and there men were for Richard's nephew Arthur, because his father Geoffrey was John's elder brother. In England a nephew had always been passed over in such cases, and John's election was quite lawful. King Philip of France took Arthur's side, but Arthur was taken by John and, there is little doubt, was murdered by him in 1202. Then Philip gathered a court of peers and declared that John had by this crime forfeited all the lands that he held of the crown of France. To carry out this decree Philip, in 1203-4, conquered all continental Normandy; only the islands clave to their duke, and they have stayed with the English kings ever since. So our Queen still holds the true Normandy, the land which remained Norman, while the rest of the duchy became French. Philip also took Anjou and the other Angevin lands; but not Aquitaine, the duchy of Queen Eleanor, who was still living. Thus John and his successors lost continental Normandy, but kept Aquitaine.

4. **Effects of the loss of Normandy.** — This final separation of England and Normandy marks one of the

chief stages in our story. If any un-English feelings still lingered in the heart of any Englishman of Norman descent, they quite died out now that England was the only country of all Englishmen, and Normandy had become a foreign and hostile land. While the first Angevin kings held their great dominion in Gaul, though England was their greatest and highest possession, we cannot say that it was in any way the head or centre, or that their other lands were dependencies of England. But now that the King of England held only the duchy of Aquitaine in the further part of Gaul, that duchy was distinctly a dependency of England, and it was always leading our kings into quarrels with France. Thus the rivalry between England and France, which began out of the union between England and Normandy, went on after Normandy was again joined to France. Thus both the foreign and the domestic position of England was fixed by the loss of Normandy. It is henceforth again a kingdom inhabited by an united English people, but a kingdom holding a large distant dependency as a fief of the French crown, and made thereby the special rival of France.

5. **The Nation and the Kings.**—It may seem strange that, just at this moment, when the chief outward signs of the Norman Conquest were swept away, and when the Normans in England had become thoroughly good Englishmen, things should in one point seem to go back. The thirteenth century, to which we have now come, is the time when the French tongue came into use for official documents. In old times men had used either English or Latin. After the Conquest English gradually died out, and for a while we have Latin only. Now French gradually comes in, and we have Latin and French. Thus, just when the English tongue was again coming to the front, it was again driven back. But this increased use of

French was a mere fashion, owing very much to the great influence which France and the French tongue had just then over all parts of Europe. And now that the whole nation was united, it was a mere fashion, and not a badge of conquest. But while the nation got more English, the kings got more foreign. John (1199-1216) filled the land with foreign mercenaries, and became the man of the Pope. The nation wrung the Great Charter from him, and this marks a great stage. Long after the Conquest, whenever there was any bad rule, men called for the law of King Edward. But now we hear no more of the law of King Edward; the Great Charter gave all that had been asked for under that name. Under John's son Henry the Third (1216-1272), the land was eaten up by strangers and plundered by the Popes. Then the nation joined together more than ever under Earl Simon of Montfort. Oddly enough, he was by birth a Frenchman in the strictest sense; but he inherited English estates, and he became a good Englishman, like King Cnut and Archbishop Anselm. Under him and under the next king Edward, (1272-1307) our national assemblies, now called *Parliaments*, began to take their present shape, with an elective House of Commons chosen by the shires and towns.

6. **King Edward the First.**—King Edward, the greatest of our later kings, and the first since the Conquest who bore an English name, was in his own day called Edward the Third or Fourth, as he really was; but afterwards he came to be called Edward the First, as the first of the name since the Conquest. Now at last we had a really English king, whose object was the greatness of England at home and abroad. He established the supremacy of England over Wales and Scotland more thoroughly than ever. Wales was now joined to England and was gradually incorporated with it; but the subjection of Scotland led

to its complete independence. Like Henry the Second, King Edward was a great lawgiver; and from his day we may say that we had got back again our old laws and freedom in shapes better suited to the times. All signs of the Norman Conquest may now be said to have passed away, except the use of the French tongue. King Edward spoke English well, and much English was written in his time; and, when he was at war with France, he gave out that the French king wished to invade England and wipe out the English tongue. Still French went on as a fashion, and became more than ever the language of official writings.

7. **The Wars with France.**—The last traces of French influence in England were finally got rid of during the great war with France which began under Edward the First's grandson Edward the Third (1327-1377). He claimed the crown of France through his mother, and a long war followed, which in 1360 was ended by the peace of Bretigny. By this Edward gave up his claim to France, but he kept the duchy of Aquitaine, the town of Calais which he had conquered, and the county of Ponthieu, not as fiefs of the crown of France, but as wholly independent dominions. Then the French broke the peace; the war began again, and England lost nearly everything except Calais, Bourdeaux, and Bayonne. But under Henry the Fifth (1413-1422) the war again began with vigour. He conquered Normandy, and made a peace by which he was to succeed to the crown of France. He died just too soon for this; but his son Henry the Sixth (1422-1460) succeeded in name to France as well as to England, and was crowned at Paris. But in his day the English were driven, first out of France, then out of Normandy, and then out of Aquitaine (1453); so that England lost both the old inheritance and the new conquest. Nothing was kept but Edward the Third's conquest of Calais, which was

not lost till 1558. These long wars became more and more, national wars of England against France. Edward the Third indeed, who had been brought up by a French mother, seems to have acted less as an English king than as a French prince claiming the French crown. But the war was quite national on the part of his subjects, and Henry the Fifth was an English king in every sense. These long wars with France naturally gave a blow to the use of French at home, as being the speech of the enemy. English quite gained the upper hand again in the course of the fourteenth century. Henry the Fifth even had ministers who could not speak French, and who therefore, in a conference with the French ministers, demanded that they should use Latin, as the common language of Western Christendom. Yet such is the power of habit that acts of parliament were written in French till quite late in the fifteenth century, and on some solemn occasions, as when the Queen gives her assent to an act of parliament, the French tongue is used still.

8. Summary.—Thus all things, the reign of Henry the First, the Angevin dominion and the break-up of that dominion, the un-English reigns of John and Henry the Third and the English reign of Edward the First, the long war with France, its victories and its defeats, all helped, in their several ways, to undo foreign influences in England and to make the land more and more English. We have in fact advanced by going back. All the best changes in our laws, institutions, and customs, have been really returns, under new forms, to our oldest ways of all. We have thus got rid of the effects of the Norman Conquest; but it has been by the help of the Norman Conquest itself that we have been able to get rid of them. The Conquest did in short give the old life and the old freedom a new start. It hindered them from dying out or going to sleep. Men had always something to strive

for and struggle against; and so we were able to keep and to reform without ever destroying and building up afresh. All this came of the special nature of the Norman Conquest of England as it was explained at the beginning. But the work was greatly helped by the fact that the Normans were after all disguised kinsmen, and it was helped still more by the personal character of their leader, by the strong will and far-seeing wisdom of William the Great himself.

August, 1884.

BOOKS

PRINTED AT

The Clarendon Press, Oxford,

AND PUBLISHED FOR THE UNIVERSITY BY

HENRY FROWDE,

AT THE OXFORD UNIVERSITY PRESS WAREHOUSE,

AMEN CORNER, LONDON.

LEXICONS, GRAMMARS, &c.

A Greek-English Lexicon, by Henry George Liddell,
D.D., and Robert Scott, D.D. *Seventh Edition.* 1883. 4to. *cloth, 1l. 16s.*

A Greek-English Lexicon, abridged from the above,
chiefly for the use of Schools. 1883. square 12mo. *cloth, 7s. 6d.*

A copious Greek-English Vocabulary, compiled from the
best authorities. 1850. 24mo. *bound, 3s.*

Graecae Grammaticae Rudimenta in usum Scholarum.
Auctore Carolo Wordsworth, D.C.L. *Nineteenth Edition,* 1882. 12mo. *cloth, 4s.*

Scheller's Lexicon of the Latin Tongue, with the German
explanations translated into English by J. E. Riddle, M.A. fol. *cloth, 1l. 1s.*

A Latin Dictionary, founded on Andrews' Edition of
Freund's Latin Dictionary. Revised, enlarged, and in great part re-written,
by Charlton T. Lewis, Ph.D., and Charles Short, LL.D. 4to. *cloth, 1l. 5s.*

A Practical Grammar of the Sanskrit Language, arranged with reference to the Classical Languages of Europe, for the use of English students. By Monier Williams, M.A. *Fourth Edition.* 8vo. *cloth, 15s.*

A Sanskrit English Dictionary, Etymologically and
Philologically arranged. By Monier Williams, M.A. 1872. 4to. *cloth, 4l. 14s. 6d.*

An Icelandic - English Dictionary, based on the MS.
collections of the late R. Cleasby. Enlarged and completed by G. Vigfusson.
4to. *cloth, 3l. 7s.*

An Anglo-Saxon Dictionary, based on the MS. collections
of the late Joseph Bosworth, D.D. Edited and enlarged by Professor T. N.
Toller, M.A., Owens College, Manchester. Parts I and II, each 15s. *To be completed in four Parts.*

An Etymological Dictionary of the English Language,
arranged on an Historical basis. By W. W. Skeat, M.A. *Second Edition.*
4to. *cloth, 2l. 4s.*

A Supplement to the First Edition of the above.
4to. 2s. 6d. *Just Published.*

A Concise Etymological Dictionary of the English
Language. By W. W. Skeat, M.A. Crown 8vo. *cloth, 5s. 6d.*

GREEK CLASSICS.

Aeschylus: Tragoediae et Fragmenta, ex recensione Guil. Dindorfii. *Second Edition*, 1851. 8vo. *cloth*, 5s. 6d.

Sophocles: Tragoediae et Fragmenta, ex recensione et cum commentariis Guil. Dindorfii. *Third Edition*, 2 vols. fcap. 8vo. *cloth*, 1l. 1s.
Each Play separately, *limp*, 2s. 6d.

The Text alone, printed on writing paper, with large margin, royal 16mo. *cloth*, 8s.

The Text alone, square 16mo. *cloth*, 3s. 6d.
Each Play separately, *limp*, 6d. (See also page 11.)

Sophocles: Tragoediae et Fragmenta, cum Annotatt. Guil. Dindorfii. Tomi II. 1849. 8vo. *cloth*, 10s.
The Text, Vol. I. 5s. 6d. The Notes, Vol. II. 4s. 6d.

Euripides: Tragoediae et Fragmenta, ex recensione Guil. Dindorfii. Tomi II. 1834. 8vo. *cloth*, 10s.

Aristophanes: Comoediae et Fragmenta, ex recensione Guil. Dindorfii. Tomi II. 1835. 8vo. *cloth*, 11s.

Aristoteles; ex recensione Immanuelis Bekkeri. Accedunt Indices Sylburgiani. Tomi XI. 1837. 8vo. *cloth*, 2l. 10s.
The volumes may be had separately (except Vol. IX.), 5s. 6d. *each*.

Aristotelis Ethica Nicomachea, ex recensione Immanuelis Bekkeri. Crown 8vo. *cloth*, 5s.

Demosthenes: ex recensione Guil. Dindorfii. Tomi IV. 1846. 8vo. *cloth*, 1l. 1s.

Homerus: Ilias, ex rec. Guil. Dindorfii. 8vo. *cloth*, 5s. 6d.

Homerus: Odyssea, ex rec. Guil. Dindorfii. 1855. 8vo. *cloth*, 5s. 6d.

Plato: The Apology, with a revised Text and English Notes, and a Digest of Platonic Idioms, by James Riddell, M.A. 1878. 8vo. *cloth*, 8s. 6d.

Plato: Philebus, with a revised Text and English Notes, by Edward Poste, M.A. 1860. 8vo. *cloth*, 7s. 6d.

Plato: Sophistes and Politicus, with a revised Text and English Notes, by L. Campbell, M.A. 1867. 8vo. *cloth*, 18s.

Plato: Theaetetus, with a revised Text and English Notes, by L. Campbell, M.A. *Second Edition*. 8vo. *cloth*, 10s. 6d.

Plato: The Dialogues, translated into English, with Analyses and Introductions. By B. Jowett, M.A. *A new Edition in five volumes*. 1875. Medium 8vo. *cloth*, 3l. 10s.

Plato: The Republic, translated into English, with an Analysis and Introduction By B. Jowett, M.A. Medium 8vo. *cloth*, 12s. 6d.

Thucydides: translated into English, with Introduction, Marginal Analysis, Notes and Indices. By the same. 2 vols. 1881. Medium 8vo. *cloth*, 1l. 12s.

THE HOLY SCRIPTURES.

The Holy Bible in the Earliest English Versions, made from the Latin Vulgate by John Wycliffe and his followers: edited by the Rev. J. Forshall and Sir F. Madden. 4 vols. 1850. royal 4to. *cloth*, 3*l*. 3*s*.

Also reprinted from the above, with Introduction and Glossary by W. W. SKEAT, M.A.

(1) **The New Testament in English**, according to the Version by John Wycliffe, about A.D. 1380, and Revised by John Purvey, about A.D. 1388. 1879. Extra fcap. 8vo. *cloth*, 6*s*.

(2) **The Book of Job, Psalms, Proverbs, Ecclesiastes,** and Solomon's Song, according to the Version by John Wycliffe. Revised by John Purvey. Extra fcap. 8vo. *cloth*, 3*s*. 6*d*.

The Holy Bible: an exact reprint, page for page, of the Authorized Version published in the year 1611. Demy 4to. *half bound*, 1*l*. 1*s*.

Novum Testamentum Graece. Edidit Carolus Lloyd, S.T.P.R., necnon Episcopus Oxoniensis. 18mo. *cloth*, 3*s*.

The same on writing paper, small 4to. *cloth*, 10*s*. 6*d*.

Novum Testamentum Graece juxta Exemplar Millianum. 18mo. *cloth*, 2*s*. 6*d*.

The same on writing paper, small 4to. *cloth*, 9*s*.

The Greek Testament, with the Readings adopted by the Revisers of the Authorised Version:—

   (1) Pica type. *Second Edition, with Marginal References.* Demy 8vo. *cloth*, 10*s*. 6*d*.

   (2) Long Primer type. Fcap. 8vo. *cloth*, 4*s*. 6*d*.

   (3) The same, on writing paper, with wide margin, *cloth*, 15*s*.

Evangelia Sacra Graece. fcap. 8vo. *limp*, 1*s*. 6*d*.

Vetus Testamentum ex Versione Septuaginta Interpretum secundum exemplar Vaticanum Romae editum. Accedit potior varietas Codicis Alexandrini. *Editio Altera.* Tomi III. 1875. 18mo. *cloth*, 18*s*.

The Oxford Bible for Teachers, containing supplementary HELPS TO THE STUDY OF THE BIBLE, including summaries of the several Books, with copious explanatory notes; and Tables illustrative of Scripture History and the characteristics of Bible Lands with a complete Index of Subjects, a Concordance, a Dictionary of Proper Names, and a series of Maps. Prices in various sizes and bindings from 3*s*. to 2*l*. 5*s*.

Helps to the Study of the Bible, taken from the OXFORD BIBLE FOR TEACHERS, comprising summaries of the several Books with copious explanatory Notes and Tables illustrative of Scripture History and the characteristics of Bible Lands; with a complete Index of Subjects, a Concordance, a Dictionary of Proper Names, and a series of Maps. Pearl 16mo. *cloth*, 1*s*.

ECCLESIASTICAL HISTORY, &c.

Baedae Historia Ecclesiastica. Edited, with English Notes, by G. H. Moberly, M.A. Crown 8vo. *cloth*, 10s. 6d.

Chapters of Early English Church History. By William Bright, D.D. 8vo. *cloth*, 12s.

Eusebius' Ecclesiastical History, according to the Text of Burton. With an Introduction by William Bright, D.D. Crown 8vo. *cloth*, 8s. 6d.

Socrates' Ecclesiastical History, according to the Text of Hussey. With an Introduction by William Bright, D.D. Crown 8vo. *cloth*, 7s. 6d.

ENGLISH THEOLOGY.

Butler's Analogy, with an Index. 8vo. *cloth*, 5s. 6d.

Butler's Sermons. 8vo. *cloth*, 5s. 6d.

Hooker's Works, with his Life by Walton, arranged by John Keble, M.A. *Sixth Edition*, 3 vols. 1874. 8vo. *cloth*, 1l. 11s. 6d.

Hooker's Works; the text as arranged by John Keble, M.A. 2 vols. 1875. 8vo. *cloth*, 11s.

Pearson's Exposition of the Creed. Revised and corrected by E. Burton, D.D. *Sixth Edition*, 1877. 8vo. *cloth*, 10s. 6d.

Waterland's Review of the Doctrine of the Eucharist, with a Preface by the present Bishop of London. 1880. crown 8vo. *cloth*, 6s. 6d.

ENGLISH HISTORY.

A History of England. Principally in the Seventeenth Century. By Leopold Von Ranke. 6 vols. 8vo. *cloth*, 3l. 3s.

Clarendon's (Edw. Earl of) History of the Rebellion and Civil Wars in England. To which are subjoined the Notes of Bishop Warburton 7 vols. 1849. medium 8vo. *cloth*, 2l. 10s.

Clarendon's (Edw. Earl of) History of the Rebellion and Civil Wars in England. 7 vols. 1839. 18mo. *cloth*, 1l. 1s.

Freeman's (E. A.) History of the Norman Conquest of England: its Causes and Results. *In Six Volumes.* 8vo. *cloth*, 5l. 9s. 6d.
    Vol. I. and II. together, *Third Edition*, 1877. 1l. 16s.
    Vol. III. *Second Edition*, 1874. 1l. 1s.
    Vol. IV *Second Edition*, 1875. 1l. 1s.
    Vol. V. 1876. 1l. 1s.
    Vol VI. Index, 1879. 10s. 6d.

Rogers's History of Agriculture and Prices in England, A.D. 1259–1793. Vols. I. and II. (1259–1400). 8vo. *cloth*, 2l. 2s.
    Vols. III. and IV. (1401–1582) 8vo. *cloth*, 2l. 10s.

Clarendon Press Series.

The Delegates of the Clarendon Press having undertaken the publication of a series of works, chiefly educational, and entitled the Clarendon Press Series, have published, or have in preparation, the following.

Those to which prices are attached are already published; the others are in preparation.

I. ENGLISH.

A First Reading Book. By Marie Eichens of Berlin; and edited by Anne J. Clough. Ext. fcap. 8vo. *stiff covers*, 4d.

Oxford Reading Book, Part I. For Little Children. Ext. fcap. 8vo. *stiff covers*, 6d.

Oxford Reading Book, Part II. For Junior Classes. Ext. fcap. 8vo. *stiff covers*, 6d.

An Elementary English Grammar and Exercise Book. By O. W. Tancock, M.A. *Second Edition.* Ext. fcap. 8vo. 1s. 6d.

An English Grammar and Reading Book, for Lower Forms in Classical Schools. By the same Author. *Fourth Edition.* Ext. fcap. 8vo. *cloth*, 3s. 6d.

Typical Selections from the best English Writers, with Introductory Notices. In Two Volumes. Extra fcap. 8vo. *cloth*, 3s. 6d. each.

The Philology of the English Tongue. By J. Earle, M.A., formerly Fellow of Oriel College, and Professor of Anglo-Saxon, Oxford. *Third Edition.* Ext. fcap. 8vo. *cloth*, 7s. 6d.

A Book for Beginners in Anglosaxon. By John Earle, M.A. *Third Edition.* Extra fcap. 8vo. *cloth*, 2s. 6d.

An Anglo-Saxon Primer, with Grammar, Notes, and Glossary. By Henry Sweet, M.A. *Second Edition.* Extra fcap. 8vo. *cloth*, 2s. 6d.

An Anglo-Saxon Reader, in Prose and Verse, with Grammatical Introduction, Notes, and Glossary. By Henry Sweet, M.A. *Fourth Edition.* Extra fcap. 8vo. *cloth*, 8s. 6d.

The Ormulum; with the Notes and Glossary of Dr. R. M. White. Edited by R. Holt, M.A. 2 vols. Extra fcap. 8vo. *cloth*, 21s.

Specimens of Early English. A New and Revised Edition. With Introduction, Notes, and Glossarial Index. By R. Morris, LL.D., and W. W. Skeat, M.A.
   Part I. From Old English Homilies to King Horn (A.D. 1150 to A.D. 1300). Extra fcap. 8vo. *cloth*, 9s.
   Part II. From Robert of Gloucester to Gower (A.D. 1298 to A.D. 1393). Extra fcap. 8vo. *cloth*, 7s. 6d.

Specimens of English Literature, from the 'Ploughmans Crede' to the 'Shepheardes Calender' (A.D. 1394 to A.D. 1579). With Introduction, Notes, and Glossarial Index. By W. W. Skeat, M.A. *Third Edition.* Ext. fcap. 8vo. *cloth*, 7s. 6d.

The Vision of William concerning Piers the Plowman,
by William Langland. Edited, with Notes, by W. W. Skeat, M.A. *Third Edition.* Ext. fcap. 8vo. *cloth*, 4s. 6d.

Chaucer. The Prioresses Tale; Sire Thopas; The
Monkes Tale; The Clerkes Tale; The Squieres Tale, &c. Edited by W. W. Skeat, M.A. *Second Edition.* Ext. fcap. 8vo. *cloth*, 4s. 6d.

Chaucer. The Tale of the Man of Lawe; The Par-
doneres Tale; The Second Nonnes Tale; The Chanouns Yemannes Tale. By the same Editor. *Second Edition.* Extra fcap. 8vo. *cloth*, 4s. 6d.

Old English Drama. Marlowe's Tragical History of Doctor Faustus, and Greene's Honourable History of Friar Bacon and Friar Bungay. Edited by A. W. Ward, M.A. Extra fcap. 8vo. *cloth*, 5s. 6d.

Marlowe. Edward II. With Notes, &c. By O. W. Tancock, M.A., Head Master of Norwich School. Extra fcap. 8vo. *cloth*, 3s.

Shakespeare. Hamlet. Edited by W. G. Clark, M.A., and W. Aldis Wright, M.A. Extra fcap. 8vo. *stiff covers*, 2s.

Shakespeare. Select Plays. Edited by W. Aldis Wright, M.A. Extra fcap. 8vo. *stiff covers.*

The Tempest, 1s. 6d. King Lear, 1s. 6d.
As You Like It, 1s. 6d. A Midsummer Night's Dream, 1s. 6d.
Julius Cæsar, 2s. Coriolanus, 2s. 6d.
Richard the Third, 2s. 6d. Henry the Fifth, 2s.
(For other Plays, see p. 7.)

Milton. Areopagitica. With Introduction and Notes. By J. W. Hales, M.A. *Third Edition.* Extra fcap. 8vo. *cloth*, 3s.

Milton. Samson Agonistes. Edited with Introduction and Notes by John Churton Collins. Extra fcap. 8vo. *stiff covers*, 1s.

Bunyan. Holy War. Edited by E. Venables, M.A. *In Preparation.* (See also p. 7.)

Addison. Selections from Papers in the Spectator. With Notes. By T. Arnold, M.A., University College. Extra fcap. 8vo. *cloth*, 4s. 6d.

Burke. Four Letters on the Proposals for Peace with the Regicide Directory of France. Edited, with Introduction and Notes, by E. J. Payne, M.A. Extra fcap. 8vo. *cloth*, 5s. *See also page 7.*

Also the following in paper covers.

Goldsmith. Deserted Village. 2d.

Gray. Elegy, and Ode on Eton College. 2d.

Johnson. Vanity of Human Wishes. With Notes by E. J. Payne, M.A. 4d.

Keats. Hyperion, Book I. With Notes by W. T. Arnold B.A. 4d.

Milton. With Notes by R. C. Browne, M.A.
Lycidas, 3d. L'Allegro, 3d. Il Penseroso, 4d.
Comus, 6d. Samson Agonistes, 6d.

Parnell. The Hermit. 2d.

Scott. Lay of the Last Minstrel. Introduction and Canto I. With Notes by W. Minto, M.A. 6d.

Clarendon Press Series. 7

A SERIES OF ENGLISH CLASSICS

Designed to meet the wants of Students in English Literature; by the late J. S. BREWER, M.A., Professor of English Literature at King's College, London.

1. **Chaucer.** The Prologue to the Canterbury Tales; The Knightes Tale; The Nonne Prestes Tale. Edited by R. Morris, LL.D. *Fifty-first Thousand.* Extra fcap. 8vo. *cloth*, 2s. 6d. See also p. 6.

2. **Spenser's Faery Queene.** Books I and II. By G. W. Kitchin, M.A. Extra fcap. 8vo. *cloth*, 2s. 6d. each.

3. **Hooker.** Ecclesiastical Polity, Book I. Edited by R. W. Church, M.A., Dean of St. Paul's. Extra fcap. 8vo. *cloth*, 2s

4. **Shakespeare.** Select Plays. Edited by W. G. Clark, M.A., and W. Aldis Wright, M.A. Extra fcap. 8vo. *stiff covers.*
    I. The Merchant of Venice. 1s. II. Richard the Second. 1s. 6d.
    III. Macbeth. 1s. 6d. (For other Plays, see p. 6.)

5. **Bacon.**
    I. Advancement of Learning. Edited by W. Aldis Wright, M.A. *Second Edition.* Extra fcap. 8vo. *cloth*, 4s. 6d.
    II. The Essays. With Introduction and Notes. By J. R. Thursfield, M.A

6. **Milton.** Poems. Edited by R. C. Browne, M.A. In Two Volumes. *Fourth Edition.* Ext. fcap. 8vo. *cloth*, 6s. 6d.
    Sold separately, Vol. I. 4s., Vol. II. 3s.

7. **Dryden.** Stanzas on the Death of Oliver Cromwell; Astraea Redux; Annus Mirabilis; Absalom and Achitophel; Religio Laici; The Hind and the Panther. Edited by W. D. Christie, M.A., Trinity College, Cambridge. *Second Edition.* Extra fcap. 8vo. *cloth*, 3s. 6d.

8. **Bunyan.** The Pilgrim's Progress, Grace Abounding, and A Relation of his Imprisonment. Edited, with Biographical Introduction and Notes, by E. Venables, M.A., Precentor of Lincoln. Extra fcap. 8vo. *cloth*, 5s.

9. **Pope.** With Introduction and Notes. By Mark Pattison, B.D., Rector of Lincoln College, Oxford.
    I. Essay on Man. *Sixth Edition.* Extra fcap. 8vo. *stiff covers*, 1s. 6d.
    II. Satires and Epistles. *Second Edition.* Extra fcap. 8vo. *stiff covers*, 2s.

10. **Johnson.** Select Works. Lives of Dryden and Pope, and Rasselas. Edited by Alfred Milnes, B.A. (Lond.), late Scholar of Lincoln College, Oxford. Extra fcap. 8vo. *cloth*, 4s. 6d.

11. **Burke.** Edited, with Introduction and Notes, by E. J. Payne, M.A., Fellow of University College, Oxford.
    I. Thoughts on the Present Discontents; the Two Speeches on America, etc. *Second Edition.* Extra fcap. 8vo. *cloth*, 4s. 6d.
    II. Reflections on the French Revolution. *Second Edition.* Extra fcap. 8vo. *cloth*, 5s. *See also p. 6.*

12. **Cowper.** Edited, with Life, Introductions, and Notes, by H. T. Griffith, B.A., formerly Scholar of Pembroke College, Oxford.
    I. The Didactic Poems of 1782, with Selections from the Minor Pieces, A.D. 1779-1783. Ext. fcap. 8vo. *cloth*, 3s.
    II. The Task, with Tirocinium, and Selections from the Minor Poems, A.D. 1784-1799. Ext. fcap. 8vo. *cloth*, 3s.

II. LATIN.

An Elementary Latin Grammar. By John B. Allen, M.A., *Third Edition.* Extra fcap. 8vo. *cloth*, 2s. 6d.

A First Latin Exercise Book. By the same Author. *Fourth Edition.* Extra fcap. 8vo. *cloth*, 2s. 6d.

A Second Latin Exercise Book. By the same Author. *In the Press.*

Reddenda Minora, or Easy Passages, Latin and Greek, for Unseen Translation. For the use of Lower Forms. Composed and selected by C. S. Jerram, M.A. Extra fcap. 8vo. *cloth*, 1s. 6d.

Anglice Reddenda, or Easy Extracts, Latin and Greek, for Unseen Translation. By C. S. Jerram, M.A. Extra fcap. 8vo. *cloth*, 2s. 6d.

Passages for Translation into Latin. Selected by J. Y. Sargent, M.A. *Sixth Edition.* Ext. fcap. 8vo. *cloth*, 2s. 6d.

First Latin Reader. By T. J. Nunns, M.A. *Third Edition.* Extra fcap. 8vo. *cloth*, 2s.

Caesar. The Commentaries (for Schools). With Notes and Maps, &c. By C. E. Moberly, M.A., Assistant Master in Rugby School.
The Gallic War. Second Edition. Extra fcap. 8vo. *cloth*, 4s. 6d.
The Civil War. Extra fcap. 8vo. *cloth*, 3s. 6d.
The Civil War. Book I. *Second Edition.* Extra fcap. 8vo. *cloth*, 2s.

Cicero. Selection of interesting and descriptive passages. With Notes. By Henry Walford, M.A. In Three Parts. *Third Edition.* Ext. fcap. 8vo. *cloth*, 4s. 6d. *Each Part separately, in limp cloth*, 1s. 6d.

Cicero. De Senectute and De Amicitia. With Notes. By W. Heslop, M.A. Extra fcap. 8vo. 2s.

Cicero. Select Letters (for Schools). With Notes. By the late C. E. Prichard, M.A., and E. R. Bernard, M.A. Extra fcap. 8vo. *cloth*, 3s.

Cicero. Select Orations (for Schools). With Notes. By J. R. King, M.A. *Second Edition.* Ext. fcap. 8vo. *cloth*, 2s. 6d.

Cornelius Nepos. With Notes, by Oscar Browning, M.A. *Second Edition.* Extra fcap. 8vo. *cloth*, 2s. 6d.

Livy. Selections (for Schools). With Notes and Maps. By H. Lee Warner, M.A. *In Three Parts.* Ext. fcap. 8vo. *cloth*, 1s. 6d. each.

Livy. Books V—VII. By A. R. Cluer, B.A. Extra fcap. 8vo. *cloth*, 3s. 6d.

Ovid. Selections for the use of Schools. With Introductions and Notes, etc. By W. Ramsay, M.A. Edited by G. G. Ramsay, M.A. *Second Edition.* Ext. fcap. 8vo. *cloth*, 5s. 6d.

Pliny. Select Letters (for Schools). With Notes. By the late C. E. Prichard, M.A., and E. R. Bernard, M.A. *Second Edition.* Extra fcap. 8vo. *cloth*, 3s.

Catulli Veronensis Liber. Iterum recognovit, apparatum criticum prolegomena appendices addidit, Robinson Ellis, A.M. 8vo. *cloth*, 16s.

Catullus. A Commentary on Catullus. By Robinson Ellis, M.A. Demy 8vo. *cloth*, 16s.

Catulli Veronensis Carmina Selecta, secundum recognitionem Robinson Ellis, A.M. Extra fcap. 8vo. *cloth*, 3s. 6d.

Cicero de Oratore. With Introduction and Notes. By A. S. Wilkins, M.A., Professor of Latin, Owens College, Manchester.
Book I. Demy 8vo. *cloth*, 6s. Book II. Demy 8vo. *cloth*, 5s.

Cicero's Philippic Orations. With Notes. By J. R. King, M.A. *Second Edition.* Demy 8vo. *cloth*, 10s. 6d.

Cicero. Select Letters. With English Introductions, Notes, and Appendices. By Albert Watson, M.A., Fellow and Lecturer of Brasenose College, Oxford. *Third Edition.* Demy 8vo. *cloth*, 18s.

Cicero. Select Letters (Text). By the same Editor. *Second Edition.* Extra fcap. 8vo. *cloth*, 4s.

Cicero pro Cluentio. With Introduction and Notes. By W. Ramsay, M.A. Edited by G. G. Ramsay, M.A., Professor of Humanity, Glasgow. *Second Edition.* Ext. fcap. 8vo. *cloth*, 3s. 6d.

Livy, Book I. By J. R. Seeley, M.A., Regius Professor of Modern History, Cambridge. *Second Edition.* Demy 8vo. *cloth*, 6s.

Horace. With Introductions and Notes. By Edward C. Wickham, M.A., Head Master of Wellington College.
Vol. I. The Odes, Carmen Seculare, and Epodes. *Second Edition.* Demy 8vo. *cloth*, 12s.

Horace. *A reprint of the above*, in a size suitable for the use of Schools. Extra fcap. 8vo. *cloth*, 5s. 6d.

Persius. The Satires. With a Translation and Commentary. By John Conington, M.A. Edited by H. Nettleship, M.A. *Second Edition.* 8vo. *cloth*, 7s. 6d.

Plautus. Trinummus. With Introductions and Notes. For the use of Higher Forms. By C. E. Freeman, M.A., and A. Sloman, M.A. Extra fcap. 8vo. *cloth*, 3s.

Sallust. With Introduction and Notes. By W. W. Capes, M.A. Extra fcap. 8vo. *cloth*, 4s. 6d. *Just Published.*

Selections from the less known Latin Poets. By North Pinder, M.A. Demy 8vo. *cloth*, 15s.

Fragments and Specimens of Early Latin. With Introduction and Notes. By John Wordsworth, M.A. Demy 8vo. *cloth*, 18s.

Tacitus. The Annals. I-VI. With Introduction and Notes. By H. Furneaux, M.A. 8vo. *cloth*, 18s.

Virgil. With Introduction and Notes. By T. L. Papillon, M.A., Fellow of New College. 2 vols. Crown 8vo. *cloth*, 10s. 6d.
The Text may be had separately, *cloth*, 4s. 6d.

A Manual of Comparative Philology, as applied to the Illustration of Greek and Latin Inflections. By T. L. Papillon, M.A., Fellow of New College. *Third Edition, Revised and Corrected.* Crown 8vo. *cloth*, 6s.

The Roman Poets of the Augustan Age. *Virgil.* By William Young Sellar, M.A. *New Edition.* 1883. Crown 8vo. 9s.

The Roman Poets of the Republic. By the same Author. Extra fcap.8vo. *cloth*, 14s.

III. GREEK.

A Greek Primer, for the use of beginners in that Language.
By the Right Rev. Charles Wordsworth, D.C.L., Bishop of St. Andrews.
Seventh Edition. Ext. fcap. 8vo. *cloth*, 1s. 6d.

Greek Verbs, Irregular and Defective. By W. Veitch.
Fourth Edition. Crown 8vo *cloth*, 10s. 6d

The Elements of Greek Accentuation (for Schools).
By H. W Chandler, M.A. Ext. fcap. 8vo. *cloth*, 2s. 6d.

A Series of Graduated Greek Readers:

First Greek Reader. By W. G. Rushbrooke, M.L.
Second Edition. Ext. fcap. 8vo. *cloth*. 2s. 6d.

Second Greek Reader. By A. J. M. Bell, M.A.
Extra fcap. 8vo. *cloth*, 3s. 6d.

Fourth Greek Reader; being Specimens of Greek Dialects. By W. W. Merry, M.A. Ext. fcap. 8vo. *cloth*, 4s. 6d.

Fifth Greek Reader. Part I, Selections from Greek Epic and Dramatic Poetry. By E. Abbott, M.A. Ext. fcap. 8vo. *cloth*, 4s. 6d.

The Golden Treasury of Ancient Greek Poetry; with Introductory Notices and Notes. By R. S. Wright, M.A. Ext. fcap. 8vo. *cloth*, 8s. 6d.

A Golden Treasury of Greek Prose; with Introductory Notices and Notes. By R. S. Wright, M.A., and J. E. L. Shadwell, M.A. Ext. fcap. 8vo. *cloth*, 4s. 6d.

Aeschylus. Prometheus Bound (for Schools). With Notes.
By A. O. Prickard, M.A. *Second Edition*. Ext. fcap. 8vo. *cloth*, 2s.

Aeschylus. Agamemnon. With Introduction and Notes.
By Arthur Sidgwick. M.A. *Second Edition*. Ext. fcap. 8vo. *cloth*, 3s.

Aristophanes. In Single Plays, edited with English Notes, Introductions, &c. By W. W. Merry, M.A. Extra fcap. 8vo.
The Clouds *Second Edition*, 2s. The Acharnians, 2s. The Frogs, 2s.

Cebetis Tabula. With Introduction and Notes by C. S. Jerram, M.A. Ext. fcap. 8vo. *cloth*, 2s. 6d.

Euripides. Alcestis (for Schools). By C. S. Jerram, M.A. Ext. fcap. 8vo. *cloth*, 2s. 6d.

Euripides. Helena. Edited with Introduction, Notes, and Critical Appendix. By the same Editor. Extra fcap. 8vo. *cloth*, 3s.

Herodotus. Selections. With Introduction, Notes, and Map. By W. W. Merry, M.A. Ext. fcap. 8vo *cloth*, 2s. 6d.

Homer. Odyssey, Books I-XII (for Schools). By W. W. Merry, M.A. *Twenty-Seventh Thousand*. Ext. fcap. 8vo. *cloth*, 4s. 6d.
Book II, separately, 1s. 6d.

Homer. Odyssey, Books XIII-XXIV (for Schools). By the same Editor. *Second Edition.* Ext. fcap. 8vo. *cloth*, 5s.

Homer. Iliad. Book I (for Schools). By D. B. Monro, M.A., Provost of Oriel College, Oxford. *Second Edition*. Ext. fcap. 8vo. *cloth*, 2s.

Homer. Iliad. Books I-XII. With an Introduction, a Brief Homeric Grammar, and Notes. By D. B. Monro, M A. Extra fcap. 8vo. *cloth*, 6s.

Homer. Iliad. Books VI and XXI. With Introduction and Notes. By Herbert Hailstone, M.A. Extra fcap 8vo. *cloth*, 1s. 6d. each.

Lucian. Vera Historia (for Schools) By C. S. Jerram, M.A. *Second Edition.* Extra fcap. 8vo. *cloth*, 1s. 6d.

Plato. Selections from the Dialogues [including the whole of the *Apology* and *Crito.*] With Introduction and Notes by J. Purves, M.A. Extra fcap. 8vo. *cloth*, 6s. 6d.

Sophocles. In Single Plays, with English Notes, &c. By Lewis Campbell, M.A., and Evelyn Abbott, M.A. Extra fcap. 8vo.
Oedipus Rex. Philoctetes. *New and Revised Edition*, 2s. each.
Oedipus Coloneus, Antigone, 1s. 9d. each.
Ajax, Electra, Trachiniae, 2s. each.

Sophocles. Oedipus Rex: Dindorf's Text, with Notes by the present Bishop of St. David's. Extra fcap. 8vo. *cloth*, 1s. 6d.

Theocritus (for Schools). With Notes. By H. Kynaston (late Snow), M.A. *Third Edition.* Ext. fcap. 8vo. *cloth*, 4s. 6d.

Xenophon. Easy Selections (for Junior Classes). With a Vocabulary, Notes, and Map. By J. S. Phillpotts, B.C.L., and C. S. Jerram, M.A. *Third Edition.* Ext. fcap. 8vo. *cloth*, 3s. 6d.

Xenophon. Selections (for Schools). With Notes and Maps. By J. S. Phillpotts, B.C.L., Head Master of Bedford School. *Fourth Edition.* Ext. fcap. 8vo. *cloth*, 3s. 6d.

Xenophon. Anabasis, Book II. With Notes and Map. By C. S. Jerram, M.A. Ext. fcap. 8vo. *cloth*, 2s.

Xenophon. Cyropaedia. Books IV, V. With Introduction and Notes. By C. Bigg, D.D. Ext. fcap. 8vo. *cloth*, 2s. 6d.

Demosthenes and Aeschines. The Orations on the Crown. With Introductory Essays and Notes. By G. A. Simcox, M.A., and W. H. Simcox, M.A. Demy 8vo. *cloth*, 12s.

Homer. Odyssey, Books I-XII. Edited with English Notes, Appendices, &c. By W. W. Merry, M.A., and the late James Riddell, M.A. Demy 8vo. *cloth*, 16s.

A Grammar of the Homeric Dialect. By D. B. Monro, M.A. Demy 8vo. *cloth*, 10s. 6d.

Sophocles. With English Notes and Introductions. By Lewis Campbell, M.A. In Two Volumes. 8vo. *each* 16s.
Vol. I. Oedipus Tyrannus. Oedipus Coloneus. Antigone. *Second Edition.*
Vol. II. Ajax. Electra. Trachiniae. Philoctetes. Fragments.

Sophocles. The Text of the Seven Plays. By the same Editor. Ext. fcap. 8vo. *cloth*, 4s. 6d.

A Manual of Greek Historical Inscriptions. By E. L. Hicks, M.A. Demy 8vo. *cloth*, 10s. 6d.

IV. FRENCH.

An Etymological Dictionary of the French Language, with a Preface on the Principles of French Etymology. By A. Brachet. Translated by G. W. Kitchin, M.A. *Third Edition.* Crown 8vo. *cloth*, 7s. 6d.

Brachet's Historical Grammar of the French Language. Translated by G. W. Kitchin, M.A. *Fifth Edition.* Ext. fcap. 8vo. *cloth*, 3s. 6d.

Clarendon Press Series.

A Short History of French Literature. By George Saintsbury. Crown 8vo. *cloth*, 10s. 6d.

Specimens of French Literature, from Villon to Hugo. Selected and arranged by George Saintsbury. Crown 8vo. *cloth*, 9s.

A Primer of French Literature. By George Saintsbury. Second Edition, with Index. Extra fcap. 8vo. *cloth*, 2s.

Corneille's Horace. Edited, with Introduction and Notes, by George Saintsbury. Ext. fcap. 8vo. *cloth*, 2s. 6d.

Molière's Les Précieuses Ridicules. Edited with Introduction and Notes. By Andrew Lang, M.A. Ext. fcap. 8vo. 1s. 6d.

Beaumarchais' Le Barbier de Séville. Edited with Introduction and Notes. By Austin Dobson. Ext. fcap, 8vo. 2s. 6d.

L'Éloquence de la Chaire et de la Tribune Françaises. Edited by Paul Blouët, B.A. Vol. I. Sacred Oratory. Ext. fcap. 8vo. *cloth*, 2s. 6d.

French Classics, Edited by GUSTAVE MASSON, B.A. *Univ. Gallic. Extra fcap. 8vo. cloth, 2s. 6d. each.*

Corneille's Cinna, and Molière's Les Femmes Savantes.

Racine's Andromaque, and Corneille's Le Menteur. With Louis Racine's Life of his Father.

Molière's Les Fourberies de Scapin, and Racine's Athalie. With Voltaire's Life of Molière.

Regnard's Le Joueur, and Brueys and Palaprat's Le Grondeur.

A Selection of Tales by Modern Writers. *Second Edition.*

Selections from the Correspondence of Madame de Sévigné and her chief Contemporaries. Intended more especially for Girls' Schools. By the same Editor. Ext. fcap. 8vo. *cloth*, 3s.

Louis XIV and his Contemporaries; as described in Extracts from the best Memoirs of the Seventeenth Century. With Notes, Genealogical Tables, etc. By the same Editor. Extra fcap. 8vo.*cloth*, 2s. 6d.

V. GERMAN.

German Classics, Edited by C. A. BUCHHEIM, *Phil. Doc., Professor in King's College, London.*

Goethe's Egmont. With a Life of Goethe, &c. *Third Edition.* Ext. fcap. 8vo. *cloth*, 3s.

Schiller's Wilhelm Tell. With a Life of Schiller; an historical and critical Introduction, Arguments, and a complete Commentary. *Sixth Edition.* Ext. fcap. 8vo. *cloth*, 3s. 6d.

—— *School Edition.* Extra fcap. 8vo. 2s. *Just Published.*

Lessing's Minna von Barnhelm. A Comedy. With a Life of Lessing, Critical Analysis, Complete Commentary, &c. *Fourth Edition.* Extra fcap. 8vo. *cloth*, 3s. 6d.

Schiller's Historische Skizzen: Egmonts Leben und Tod, and Belagerung von Antwerpen. *Second Edition.* Ext. fcap. 8vo. *cloth*, 2s. 6d.

Goethe's Iphigenie auf Tauris. A Drama. With a Critical Introduction and Notes. *Second Edition.* Ext. fcap. 8vo. *cloth*, 3s.

Clarendon Press Series. 13

Modern German Reader. A Graduated Collection of Prose
Extracts from Modern German Writers:—
Part I. With English Notes, a Grammatical Appendix, and a complete Vocabulary. *Third Edition.* Extra fcap. 8vo. *cloth*, 2s. 6d.

Lessing's Nathan der Weise. With Introduction, Notes, etc.
Extra fcap. 8vo. *cloth*, 4s. 6d.

Halm's Griseldis. In Preparation.

LANGE'S *German Course.*

The Germans at Home; a Practical Introduction to
German Conversation, with an Appendix containing the Essentials of German Grammar. *Second Edition.* 8vo. *cloth*, 2s. 6d.

The German Manual; a German Grammar, a Reading
Book, and a Handbook of German Conversation. 8vo. *cloth*, 7s. 6d.

A Grammar of the German Language. 8vo. *cloth*. 3s. 6d.

German Composition; a Theoretical and Practical Guide
to the Art of Translating English Prose into German. 8vo. *cloth*, 4s. 6d.

Lessing's Laokoon. With Introduction, English Notes, &c.
By A. Hamann, Phil. Doc., M.A. Ext. fcap. 8vo. *cloth*, 4s. 6d.

Wilhelm Tell. By Schiller. Translated into English Verse
by Edward Massie, M.A. Ext. fcap. 8vo. *cloth*, 5s.

VI. MATHEMATICS, &c.

Figures made Easy: a first Arithmetic Book. (Introductory to 'The Scholar's Arithmetic.') By Lewis Hensley, M.A., formerly Fellow of Trinity College, Cambridge. Crown 8vo. *cloth*, 6d.

Answers to the Examples in Figures made Easy.
By the same Author. Crown 8vo. *cloth*, 1s.

The Scholar's Arithmetic. By the same Author. Crown 8vo. *cloth*, 4s. 6d.

The Scholar's Algebra. By the same Author. Crown 8vo. *cloth*, 4s. 6d.

Book-keeping. By R. G. C. Hamilton and John Ball.
New and enlarged Edition. Ext. fcap. 8vo. *limp cloth*, 2s.

Acoustics. By W. F. Donkin, M.A., F.R.S., Savilian Professor of Astronomy, Oxford. Crown 8vo. *cloth*, 7s. 6d.

A Treatise on Electricity and Magnetism. By J. Clerk
Maxwell, M.A., F.R.S. A New Edition, edited by W. D. Niven, M.A. 2 vols. Demy 8vo. *cloth*, 1l. 11s. 6d.

An Elementary Treatise on Electricity. By James Clerk
Maxwell, M.A. Edited by William Garnett, M.A. Demy 8vo. *cloth*, 7s. 6d.

A Treatise on Statics. By G. M. Minchin, M.A. *Second
Edition, Revised and Enlarged.* Demy 8vo. *cloth*, 14s.

Uniplanar Kinematics of Solids and Fluids. By G. M.
Minchin, M.A., Crown 8vo. *cloth*, 7s. 6d.

Geodesy. By Colonel Alexander Ross Clarke, R.E. Demy
8vo. *cloth*, 12s. 6d.

XI. ART, &c.

A Handbook of Pictorial Art. By R. St. J. Tyrwhitt, M.A. *Second Edition.* 8vo. *half morocco,* 18s.

A Treatise on Harmony. By Sir F. A. Gore Ouseley, Bart., M.A., Mus. Doc. *Third Edition.* 4to. *cloth,* 10s.

A Treatise on Counterpoint, Canon, and Fugue, based upon that of Cherubini. By the same Author. *Second Edition.* 4to. *cloth,* 16s.

A Treatise on Musical Form, and General Composition. By the same Author. 4to. *cloth,* 10s.

A Music Primer for Schools. By J. Troutbeck, M.A., and R. F. Dale, M.A., B. Mus. *Second Edition.* Crown 8vo. *cloth,* 1s. 6d.

The Cultivation of the Speaking Voice. By John Hullah. *Second Edition.* Extra fcap. 8vo. *cloth,* 2s. 6d.

XII. MISCELLANEOUS.

Text-Book of Botany, Morphological and Physiological. By Dr. Julius Sachs, Professor of Botany in the University of Würzburg. *Second Edition.* Edited, with an Appendix, by Sydney H. Vines, M.A. Royal 8vo. *half morocco,* 1l. 11s. 6d.

A System of Physical Education: Theoretical and Practical. By Archibald Maclaren, The Gymnasium, Oxford. Extra fcap. 8vo. *cloth,* 7s. 6d.

An Icelandic Prose Reader, with Notes, Grammar, and Glossary. By Dr. Gudbrand Vigfusson and F. York Powell, M.A. Extra fcap. 8vo. *cloth,* 10s. 6d.

Dante. Selections from the Inferno. With Introduction and Notes. By H. B. Cotterill, B.A. Extra fcap. 8vo. *cloth,* 4s. 6d.

Tasso. La Gerusalemme Liberata. Cantos I, II. By the same Editor. Extra fcap. 8vo. *cloth,* 2s. 6d.

A Treatise on the Use of the Tenses in Hebrew. By S. R. Driver, M.A., Fellow of New College. *New and Enlarged Edition.* Extra fcap. 8vo. *cloth,* 7s. 6d.

Outlines of Textual Criticism applied to the New Testament. By C. E. Hammond, M.A., Fellow and Tutor of Exeter College, Oxford. *Third Edition.* Extra fcap. 8vo. *cloth,* 3s. 6d.

A Handbook of Phonetics, including a Popular Exposition of the Principles of Spelling Reform. By Henry Sweet, M.A. Extra fcap. 8vo. *cloth,* 4s. 6d.

The Student's Handbook to the University and Colleges of Oxford. *Seventh Edition.* Extra fcap. 8vo. *cloth,* 2s. 6d.

The DELEGATES OF THE PRESS *invite suggestions and advice from all persons interested in education; and will be thankful for hints, &c., addressed to the* SECRETARY TO THE DELEGATES, *Clarendon Press, Oxford.*

www.ingramcontent.com/pod-product-compliance
Lightning Source LLC
Chambersburg PA
CBHW032154160426
43197CB00008B/904